TWAYNE'S WORLD AUTHORS SERIES

A Survey of the World's Literature

Sylvia E. Bowman, Indiana University

GENERAL EDITOR

AUSTRALIA

Joseph Jones, University of Texas, Austin

EDITOR

Henry Handel Richardson
(Ethel Florence Lindesay Richardson)

TWAS 366

Photo courtesy of the National Library, Canberra

Henry Handel Richardson

HENRY HANDEL RICHARDSON

(Ethel Florence Lindesay Richardson)

By WILLIAM D. ELLIOTT

Bemidji State University

TWAYNE PUBLISHERS

A DIVISION OF G. K. HALL & CO., BOSTON

823.9
R522E
1975

Library of Congress Cataloging in Publication Data

Elliott, William D   1938–
    Henry Handel Richardson (Ethel Florence Lindesay
Richardson)

    (Twayne's world authors series; TWAS 366: Australia)
    Bibliography: pp. 159–72
    Includes index.
    1. Richardson, Henry Handel, pseud.
PR9619.3.R5Z65   823 [B]   75–12692
ISBN 0–8057–6217–5

This book is dedicated to my wife, Gwen, a constant source of help and encouragement; to Professor Joe Lee Davis, who, as my dissertation chairman and instructor at the University of Michigan, provided lifelong ideals for the young scholar; and to my mother and father, whose 1960 research trip to Canberra in the name of science and whose continual support inspired my first interest in Australia.

Contents

About the Author

Dr. William D. Elliott, Associate Professor of English at Minnesota's Bemidji State University, began his interest in Australian literature at The University of Michigan. After completing his doctoral dissertation on "The Fortunes of Richard Mahony" in 1967, he published articles on Richardson and Commonwealth Literature in *Studies in the Novel, Discourse, Ann Arbor Review*, and *Minnesota English Journal*. A Spring, 1974 sabbatical leave to England and Australia, supported in part by the American Philosophical Society, enabled him to study the Richardson papers at the National Library in Canberra, visit the Richardson Memorial in Chiltern, and talk with Australian critics and poets. His stay in England included a visit with Miss Olga Roncoroni, Richardson's literary executrix.

Dr. Elliott's interest in Richardson as a writer also stems from active publication of his own fiction and poetry. A short story appeared on Martha Foley's list of Distinguished Fiction for 1969; a novella, "Stopping off in Switzerland," won the 1968 McKnight Foundation Humanities Award; poems have appeared in over seventy periodicals, including *Epoch, Windsor Review, The Carleton Miscellany*, and *Southern Humanities Review*. He also won Hopwood Awards while at The University of Michigan, and has an M.F.A. in Creative Writing from The University of Iowa.

His interests are now divided between critical and creative writing. A State University Faculty Research Grant led to research and completion of a novel. His recent contacts with Australian poets have interested him in writing a critical book of those younger poets less known in America.

Preface

This critical study will attempt to reveal Henry Handel Richardson as the first Australian realistic novelist to develop a multi-dimensional single character in an extended work of fiction. She advanced the Australian novel through searching explorations of human vulnerability by setting a romantic hero in a comprehensively realistic context; and, in doing so, successfully fused two visions of man in literature.

Since her life forms the tools for most of her fiction, chapter 1 focuses in detail on the chief events and suggests their uses in her writing. Chapter 2 analyzes the important part her early translations of Jacobsen and Björnson play in shaping her literary method, and each of the succeeding chapters analyze her fiction from *Maurice Guest* (1908) to *The Young Cosima* (1939). Special attention is given to her trilogy, *The Fortunes of Richard Mahony* (collected edition, 1930), as the most representative example of her ability to build a multidimensional character. The concluding chapter will both summarize this development through each of the novels and discuss current literary scholarship: one critical school that condemns Richardson for her "literal-mindedness" and the other that defends her imaginative use of historical and autobiographical materials.

Writing about Henry Handel Richardson has been in the most complete sense a scholar's adventure. Since she was born in Australia, studied on the Continent, and lived most of her adult life in England, attempts were made to follow her creative path and to study the most recent materials available in the Australian National Library in Canberra, the depository library. She emerges as a complex writer, occasionally labeled Anglo-Australian, yet unquestionably the author of a great Australian trilogy which required an intimate knowledge of the Australia she left as a young girl. She is also the author of a great novel influenced by continental models and the writer of one of English literature's most penetrating school novels, *The Getting of Wisdom.* She is also, I quickly discovered by way of interview, at this moment the center of a literary reevaluation that has taken on the character of a small war about the nature of her contribution to Australian letters.

My adventure began as a doctoral student at The University of Michigan, where due to the thanks of my dissertation chairman Professor Joe Lee Davis, I was led to undertake a critical reappraisal of *The Fortunes of Richard Mahony.* Correspondence with Professor Joseph Jones, Field Editor of the Twayne World Authors' Series, guided me through sabbatical study in England and Australia, where the story of the genius of Henry Handel Richardson gradually began to unfold. I am indebted to Professor Jones.

In England I owe special thanks for interviews with Olga M. Roncoroni, literary executrix to the Richardson Estate; Elizabeth Anderson, Copyrights Editor for William Heinemann and Company; and Mr. Donald Simpson, Librarian, The Royal Commonwealth Society, London. The libraries of the Commonwealth Institute of the University of London, the British Museum, Australia House, the Bodleian Library of Oxford University, and the School of Commonwealth Studies at the University of Leeds require special thanks, as does Professor William Walsh, Director of the Commonwealth Program at Leeds, with whom I had a brief talk. Correspondence with Dorothy Green was of particular value. Her willingness to allow me to quote freely from her magnificent study *Ulysses Bound* was of incalculable help.

In Australia my special thanks must go to Professor Leonie Kramer, who not only talked with me in Canberra but spent a great deal of time tracking down sources during my stay at the Department of English, University of Sydney; thanks also go to Miss Suzanne Mourot, Librarian of the Mitchell Library, and Mrs. Elizabeth Loder Webby. I must also thank Mrs. Pauline Fanning, Chief Librarian, Australian Studies, and Mr. Palmer, Manuscripts Librarian, of The Australian National Library at Canberra for their considerate help. Special thanks also go to Professor John Hardy, Chairman, Department of English, Australian National University, Dr. Nina Christesen, Professor Manning Clarke, Professor A. D. Hope, Mrs. Judith Wright

Preface

McKinney, and Dr. Liviae Dobrez, who supplied encouragement, intelligent conversation, and interest in my project. At Melbourne, I wish to particularly thank Professor Vincent Buckley, Chris Wallace-Crabbe, Dr. C. B. Christesen, Weston Bate of the University of Melbourne, and Kathleen Fitzpatrick.

This work was supported in part by a grant from the American Philosophical Society.

My thanks must also go to Bemidji State University for a ten week sabbatical leave to do the preliminary research. I want to thank, as well, the staff of the A. C. Clark Library for their efficient gathering of photocopy and interlibrary loan materials. Special thanks go to Mrs. Mary Kay Smith, Assistant Reference Librarian. And finally my deepest appreciation to my wife Gwen, who typed the manuscript for publication, compiled the index, and gave me constant encouragement.

WILLIAM D. ELLIOTT

Bemidji State University

Chronology

1870 Henry Handel Richardson born January 3 at Blanche Terrace, 139 Victoria Parade, East Melbourne.

1875 Residence in Hawthorn, a suburb of Melbourne, after a grand tour of Europe and a loss of the family's fortunes. She remembers constant family arguments over money.

1876 Residence in Chiltern, "Lake View," Victoria, where Ethel gains her first view of the Australian countryside and remembers the smell of wattles. The beginning of her father's physical and mental deterioration.

1877 Residence in Queenscliffe, Victoria, where her father, in failing health, is appointed acting health officer and acting tide surveyor. Young Ethel gains her love for the sea.

1878 After an apoplectic attack, Dr. Richardson is admitted to the Cremorne Private Asylum in Richmond, Melbourne on September 11; three months later he is transferred to the government asylum at Yarra Bend. To support the family, Mrs. Richardson is appointed postmistress in the village of Koroit, in the remote western district of Victoria. Ethel's memories of Koroit are distasteful.

1879 After several months in the family care at Koroit, Dr. Richardson dies on August 1 and is buried facing the sea at Tower Hill cemetery, some three miles from Koroit. Ethel remembers only childhood relief.

1880 Residence at Maldon; childhood infatuation with the local Vicar, Jack Stretch.

1883– Attendance at the Ladies Presbyterian College, Melbourne,
1887 later to form the setting for her novel, *The Getting of Wisdom.*

1886 Ethel wins the Senior Pianoforte Scholarship, performs at the Annual Concert, is commended personally by the governor's wife and encouraged to seek further study by the famous Hungarian musician Edward Remenyi.

1887 Ethel wins First Class Honors in Senior English and history; forms friendship with Constance Bulteel whom she meets later in London and corresponds with for the rest of her life.

1888   Ethel teaches unsuccessfully as a morning governess for a few months in Toorak. On August 3, Ethel, Lilian, and their mother sail for England on the *Ormuz*.

1889   At Easter, Ethel begins her study in the Leipzig Conservatory after brief visits with relatives in Northamptonshire and Cambridge.

1892   The March 25 *Programme Conservatorium* marks Ethel's accomplishments as a musician at Leipzig. She tells Shreck and Weidenbock, her two piano instructors, that she wishes to stop her studies because of her engagement to John G. Robertson, a young student at Leipzig completing a doctorate in German literature.

1894   Ethel writes an essay imitating Lamb, "Christmas in Australia," and a defense of Ibsen's *The Masterbuilder* for a manuscript magazine begun by one of her old shipmates aboard the *Ormuz*.

1895   Marries J. G. Robertson in Dublin, on December 20. On June 13 "Music Study in Leipzig" is published in *The Lady*.

1896   First books published, by Heinemann of London: a translation of J. P. Jacobsen's *Niels Lyhne* and Björnson's *The Fisher Lass*.

1897   Ethel and her husband move to Strasbourg on September 25, where her husband has been appointed lecturer. Ethel begins work on *Maurice Guest*. Her mother's death in November has a profound effect on her and later creates the impetus for the short story "Mary Christina." An article, "The Shubert Centenary," is published in *The Speaker* on January 30 and "Ibsen in Translation," an attack on William Archer's translation of *John Gabriel Borkman*, is published in the July 10 issue. An article on Jacobsen entitled "A Danish Poet" had been published in November.

1901   From January through March 8, substantial progress on *Maurice Guest* is recorded in her Diary, including "Maurice and Louise. End Chapters."

1903   On September 13, Robertson's *History of German Literature* is published. Dr. Robertson appointed to the Chair
of German Literature at The University of London, and
on April 19 the Robertsons leave for 5 Lyon Road, Harrow-
on-the-Hill.

1908   *Maurice Guest* is published in August by William Heinemann.

1910   *The Getting of Wisdom* published.

1912   A two week stay in Australia to check facts for *Australia
Felix.*

1917   *Australia Felix* published; completed in 1915 but delayed
by her publisher because of World War I.

1925   *The Way Home* published with a small sale. With the
death of William Heinemann in 1921, her chief supporter
and promoter is now gone.

1929   *Ultima Thule* published January 9, at her husband's
expense, since Heinemann refuses to publish any more
Richardson work because of financial losses on *The Way
Home.* After Gerald Gould's review and other major
London critics, publishing expenses are returned to Robertson and Heinemann issues five impressions each succeeding month. *Ultima Thule* is published by Norton in
the United States and becomes a book-club choice which
sells eighty thousand copies the first month.

1930   *The Fortunes of Richard Mahony* is published in a collected edition. "The Story of Wagner and von Bülow—
and the Women Behind Their Music" is published in the
Radio Times on August 29. Henry Handel Richardson is
awarded the Australian Gold Medal for Literature.

1931   *Two Studies* is published by Ulysses Press of London in
a limited edition.

1932   Henry Handel Richardson nominated for the Nobel Prize.

1933   Professor Robertson dies; Ethel moves to "Green Ridges,"
Sussex, where she remains until her death.

1934   *The End of a Childhood* published, including four chapters in the continuing life of the Mahonys.

1939   *The Young Cosima* published.

1940   An uncollected short story, "The Coat," published in *Good
Housekeeping* in February. "Some Notes on my Books"

published in the *Virginia Quarterly Review* summer issue.

1942 Four chapters finished of a novel on London low life tentatively entitled *Nick and Sanny*; instructions to Olga Roncoroni were to destroy the manuscript if Richardson never lived to finish it. "Autobiographical Sketch" published in *Twentieth Century Authors*, New York.

1946 Henry Handel Richardson dies at Green Ridges, on March 30.

1948 *Myself When Young*, her unfinished autobiography, published in London and America.

1950 "Sister Ann," an uncollected short story, appears in *Woman's Day* on May 22.

1970 "Lake View" in Chiltern, Victoria, is created as the Henry Handel Richardson Memorial by the National Trust of Australia.

CHAPTER 1

Life

I *Parental Background*

ALL of the writing of Henry Handel Richardson has come out of the psychological depths of her family experience. For this reason, some examination of her life is essential to an understanding of her books. Born Ethel Florence Lindesay Richardson at Blanche Terrace, 139 Victoria Parade in East Melbourne on January 3, 1870,[1] her autobiography begins with an account of her father:

> My father, Walter Lindesay Richardson, was a native of Dublin, the descendant of two Irish families, the Lindesays and the Richardsons, who had intermarried in the eighteenth century. He was the youngest child of my grandfather's second marriage—at the age of seventy-two to a girl of eighteen—and, by the time he grew up, the wild sons of the first marriage had contrived to run through the family inheritance. After one or two attempts at settling down to a dull country practice, he was bitten by the prevailing unrest, and emigrated to Australia in the hope of digging up a fortune. The usual disappointments following, he turned back to medicine, prospered, and in his early forties was able to retire from practice as a fairly well-to-do man.[2]

Many biographical accounts of Richardson overemphasize the mother-centered household and the disabled father, while Richardson herself begins her autobiography with a picture of him. More important, it is a portrait of a man who was much more than the victim of indecision and sensitivity, and much more the prosperous, responsible doctor, as the records of his life in medicine indicate.[3]

The course of Dr. Richardson's life until the birth of his daughter has often been portrayed as an imaginative mixture of the

Richard Mahony of the trilogy and its author, Henry Handel Richardson. Walter Richardson's colonel father died when he was only nine months old, leaving him in the care of what has been described as a tender, overprotective, forceful mother.[4] Mrs. Neustatter's account, probably the most comprehensive, describes Walter's mother as "an Irish Protestant who lived in Dublin and saw Roman Catholicism and priests as Devil's work. In later life she was obsessively religious, belligerently Protestant."[5] In *The Way Home*, as Richard Mahony visits his mother in Ireland, he is told: "My beloved son, colony life is disastrous. It ruins the soul . . . as it ruins the body."[6] As part of a strongly Protestant family, Walter was actively religious, but his commitment from the beginning was more reflective, and he took nothing for granted. As a child, he became emotionally close to his mother but never to her second husband, Dr. Bayne Cheyne. His mother's marriage brought about their move to Edinburgh. As a number of critics have observed, an Oedipal relationship to his mother could have easily developed, resulting in a sensitiveness of personality and a desire to escape—personality traits that were used so effectively by his daughter in the trilogy.

His choice of the medical profession was a combination of factors: (1) an interest in following his stepfather in order to please his mother; (2) the concern for relieving suffering, which appealed to his strong social sense; (3) his absorption with intellectual questions, which might have easily led him to devote his life to research (to which he was perhaps more suited) rather than to the practice of medicine; and (4) the necessity of making a living, as mentioned by Henry Handel Richardson in *Myself When Young*. His absorption with things of the mind and spirit—philosophy, religious studies, spiritualism, and astrology—so clearly displayed in the trilogy, often runs in direct contrast to his profession as a general practitioner, where daily human contacts were so important.

His training in medicine at the University of Edinburgh continued these conflicting interests. At the time of his graduation in August, 1859, the university was a center for the study of physiology, animal magnetism, phrenology, and mesmerism.[7] Two professors—William Gregory and Karl von Reichenbach—

had a lasting effect on his intellectual investigations into spiritualism. Reichenbach theorized that a force resting between heat, light, and electricity explained the phenomena of animal magnetism, which often became the "bridge" for belief in spiritualism by the leading intellectuals, scientists, and doctors of the day in Australia and elsewhere.[8]

Dr. Richardson was also exposed to the most advanced techniques in obstetrics of the 1840s. As the pupil of James Young Simpson, he witnessed the first use of chloroform anesthesia in childbirth in 1847. He regularly attended surgery and midwifery, and the sessions of the university's distinguished pathologist, Professor Henderson. Henderson passed on to his students his adherence to homeopathy—the use of drugs to induce states of disease for experimentation—and until 1867 Walter Richardson supported his professor's thesis. He was admitted as a Fellow of the Royal College of Surgeons shortly after graduation. During his years as a medical student, none of the traits of instability, hypersensitivity, or unsociability typical of the fictional Richard Mahony appear in the records.[9]

Walter Richardson's medical practice began with brief hospital appointments in Edinburgh and Wales, followed by an assistant practitioner's position in Kent. By some unexplained confusion,[10] he was found guilty of medical neglect by a local board of guardians, and learning of the Australian goldfields, he shipped out for the Ballarat gold diggings in June, 1852, to recover the family fortunes spent recklessly by the elder sons of his dead father.[11] Since the goldfields did not prove prosperous, he opened up a general store. During his four years on the goldfields, first as digger then as shopkeeper, he was active in public life, contrary to the pictures in the trilogy. He joined the Masonic order of Ballarat and participated in the foundation-stone laying ceremony of the Ballarat Hospital on Christmas Day, 1855. He married Mary Bailey in Geelong on August 27, 1855, and a year later registered with the Medical Board of Victoria to practice medicine.[12]

Henry Handel Richardson's mother, Mary Bailey, was English, the daughter of a Leicester solicitor. Her mother's family had been engaged in farming. At the age of fourteen she left Leicester to join a brother in Melbourne. Mary Bailey was a study in contrast to her husband: easily adaptable to Australia, of English yeoman stock, practical-minded, and completely capable of the day-to-day adjustments required of emigrants in a rapidly emerging country. The Baileys and the Richardsons seem to form a study in contrasts in most aspects. The autobiography points out that her mother's "... talents were purely practical; there was little she could not do with her large, capable hands ... her natural bent may have been for mechanics, a field entirely closed, of course, to women of her day."[13]

While the Richardsons and Baileys were of utterly different temperaments, the marriage, medical practice, intellectual pursuits, and financial resources flourished by the time of Henry Handel's birth. By 1862 the Ballarat directory gives the Richardson residence as the north side of Webster Street—near the solicitors and Dr. Bunce, another doctor of the town. The next year Henry Handel Richardson's father was named honorary medical officer to the Ballarat District Hospital and in 1866 received the forty-first medical degree from the University of Melbourne granted *ad eundum gradum,* which was followed by his election to the University Senate. His midwifery register indicates over one hundred babies delivered per annum.[14] He wrote a number of articles for the leading medical journals of the day, was a personal friend of the Government Botanist, was elected honorary member of the Medical Society of Victoria, was founding member of the Australian Health Society, and in 1866 was a subscribing member and correspondent for the Medical Benevolent Association of Victoria. He was the first president of the Victorian Association of Progressive Spiritualists and spoke so eloquently on "Spiritualism in Australia" while in London that "the English Spiritualists Association ... tried to retain him as an official lecturer."[15] All of this is essential to understanding how Henry Handel Richardson transformed her father's life into a fictional failure, never equal to life's demands, who from the beginning was often irritable, moody, and ineffective.

During his first trip to England in 1867, three years before his daughter's birth, he indicated none of the personality traits resulting from a syphilitic infection that he had contracted during his twenties, either on the 1852 emigration by ship from

England to Australia, or on the Ballarat goldfields before his marriage.[16] Upon returning from England in 1869, his financial resources from investments in stocks allowed him to retire from active practice until 1874. Examples from his account book show dividends of 1104.9.9 pounds in 1868, with an escalating annual income in the next four years. Receipts and expenditures always show a surplus of from 280 to 488 pounds.[17] The birth of Ethel Florence, their first child, is described by the author as "amid the crashings of a terrific thunderstorm." Richardson notes that her parents had "almost given up hope of a family, and I was passionately welcomed, for my mother adored children."[18]

Until the grand tour of Europe, three years later, her father was elected to the exclusive Yorick Club of Melbourne, and became intensely involved in social and cultural pursuits. The family lived in Chapel Street, St. Kilda, in a nine-room brick home near Mary's brother, who had now become a successful politician and businessman—the John Turnham of the trilogy. A second daughter was born in April, 1871, at the St. Kilda House.

II *Early Years*

When Ethel was three, her father[19] was prosperous enough to take the family to Europe. She traveled with her sister and parents on *The Red Jacket* to England, where they stayed in Kensington, London, and at the house of an uncle, Henry Richardson, near Cork, Ireland. As the friend and critic Nettie Palmer writes, "they made the Grand Tour of Europe, in the Victorian way, though Ethel, . . . remembered little of the experience. Yet it is probable that it complicated her mind throughout her childhood (as it complicated Cuffy's in *The Way Home*) by laying up a store of pictures she could not quite account for—pictures that might be either fact or dream, flashing as they did into consciousness when some hidden spring was touched."[20]

Her father was busy lecturing to spiritualist organizations. On July, 1873, he lectured in London's fashionable Cavendish rooms. A London meeting with Count Alexandre Aksakov of St. Petersburg attracted an audience of eight hundred. Such events were typical of his activities in England. His daughter's autobiography tells us: "From a house in Kensington I carry away my earliest

picture of my father, or rather of the dressing-gown he wore—
a light grey piped with red—as he sat at breakfast reading *The
Times*."[21] Such a picture—distant, yet prosperous and content—
contrasts radically with her childhood memories of him after
the onset of the syphilitic infection.

Leaving the children with the Henry Richardsons in Cork,
her parents toured the Continent with much the same extrava-
gance and energy that they displayed in England. Upon arriving in Italy, they learned that their financial resources as mining
speculators were lost—a not unusual circumstance among the
"bubble companies" in the early 1870s. Rapid reverses of fortunes and spectacular crashes on the stock market were the
result of a number of factors, including particularly unscrupulous
agents and lawsuits between mining companies. Typical of the
mining company disputes during the period was a triangular
lawsuit between "the united Hand in Hand and Band of Hope,
and the Koh-I-Noor Companies." This was a battle over regis-
tration rights and the last company involved—the Koh-I-Noor—
was one in which Walter Richardson (and Richard Mahony)
held investments.[22]

Returning to Australia by the overland route, Richardson left
his family to return alone aboard the *Sobraon,* while he began a
practice and built a house in Hawthorn, a sparsely populated
suburb of Melbourne. Henry Handel Richardson remembers
the trip as a four year old, engrossed in her early acquired habits
of reading "volumes of *Chatterbox* and *Little Folks*" and—
"judging by later experiences I can imagine feeling quite sorry
when the voyage of eighty odd days was over, and my father
came on board at Queenscliffe, to sail with us up the Bay to
Melbourne. Compared with my mother's his absence meant little
to us as children."[23] Her memories reflect the beginnings of a
physical and psychological dislocation that was to influence
both her "hatred" of her father's illness in Koroit and, much
later in life, her desire to tell his story.

Three significant recollections stand out—her four and five
year old's hatred of the "dark and Poky" furnished house in a
terrace adjoining the Fitzroy gardens, the illnesses and quarrels
over clothes she had with her mother, and the overheard debates
between her parents about money after moving into the furni-

ture-barren Hawthorn house in 1875. But other recollections stand out that correlate exactly with her adulthood commitment to the arts—a gift of a book from her father's nephew and her first piano lessons. And music, from the beginning, seemed to be a natural talent:

. . . my sister and I seem to have come into the world with an instinctive sense for notes and tones; and on being introduced to music, in the shape of a piano, took to it just like ducks to water. We quickly learned all my mother could teach us; and soon outstripped her in the playing of her hardest pieces. . . .[24]

By her sixth birthday, the Richardsons had moved to a small practice in Chiltern, Northern Victoria. The reasons for the move are complex. Certainly the failing practice at Hawthorn and debts accumulated from the purchase of the Hawthorn house were significant. But Walter Richardson's illness also played an important part. His letters to his wife, as well as medical studies, indicate the first symptoms of syphilis. Specifically, clear structural damage to the brain and nervous system became the last effect of the syphilitic organism, the spirochete,[25] later to be recorded by Richardson in *Ultima Thule*, the last volume of her trilogy.

Typical of his letters that reveal a precise medical description include an early July, 1877, letter: "I had frequent fits of giddiness which made me reel like a drunken man . . . there must be something wrong inside my head. . . ."[26]

Or the following:

I was just up at Mandy posting a letter and I found myself unable to articulate—I could not say what I wanted, I am very uneasy about myself I lay down. I said I thought it was a faint I said I had been out in the sun—I am afraid it is something worse—I have been so distressed about the practice I fear it has upset me—I am going in to lie down.[27]

Both the syntax and the content of the letters, much of which is preserved in *Ultima Thule*, indicate that the headaches, tremors, vertigo, and depression initiated Walter Richardson's

move to Queenscliffe as acting health officer in 1877. But there
were other factors. The Frost letters in the National Library's
collection reveal that Chiltern, as a small, isolated town in
the 1930s had "the same hostility of the '70's . . . thinly veiled to
any strangers with an alien feeling to the town. . . ."[28] Frank
Frost, an owner of Lakeview (the Richardson home) in 1930–31,
wrote a number of startling letters to Henry Handel Richardson after he read her description of it in *Ultima Thule*. He describes the resentment of the town after reading her account
of it. But newer residents, like the Frosts, felt "how vividly
genuine to the life here the story is. . . . One is bound to stop
many times and say 'exactly true.' "[29] Such recently uncovered
correspondence tends to indicate that it was a *combination* of
Richardson's failing health and a somewhat isolated, insular,
provincial community that brought about the rapid failure at
Chiltern. My observations of the town in 1974 would confirm
this. Yet Henry Handel Richardson writes that

quite the most vivid and lasting impression Chiltern left on me,
however, was one of colour and scent. Our governess adventured with
us beyond our township, out into the bush, and there, for the first
time, I saw and smelt wattles in bloom. It was an unforgettable experience. To this day, I have only to catch a whiff of mimosa in a
dingy London street and I am once more a small girl, sitting on a
fallen tree under the bluest of skies, with all around me those golden,
almost stupefyingly sweet masses of blossom.[30]

This sensation is carefully developed in Cuffy, the young Mahony
boy who, after the death of both of his parents in *The End of
Childhood,* is reassured by the smell of wattles as he leaves
his last home.

Despite his failing health, Richardson was also appointed acting tide surveyor at Queenscliffe, a job that involved the inspec-
tion of incoming ships. Unhappily, this task emphasized the
results of his damaged nervous system, which included loss of
muscular control and coordination, an atoxic gait, and the numb-
ing of the lower body. The spirochetal invasion of his spinal
cord and ganglia was nearly complete,[31] to be followed by an
epileptic attack. All this is carefully and painstakingly recorded

in *Ultima Thule*—the epileptic attack combined with Mahony's starting a fire in his surgery to burn what became to him the hated receipts and bonds, the "money."

In contrast, Richardson's autobiographical account is less spectacular: "Our day was given up to bathing, or playing on the beach. Thanks to my father, who was determined that two rather pale and peaky children should reap the full benefit of sea and sea-air."[32] Or this account of her father's buying books:

In Queenscliffe my father once more found himself within visiting distance of the Melbourne bookshops; and though he was now a poor man the old passion proved too strong for him. I became the happy possessor, amongst other things, of fine editions of *The Pilgrim's Progress* and *Robinson Crusoe*, copiously illustrated. . . . I can also recall my father setting me down to passages in Scott's novels that he thought might interest an eight year old. Had he lived, I should certainly have profited by his guidance. As it was, after he went, my taste ran riot; I simply read every and any book I could get.[33]

Her memories of his illness provide further contrasts with the trilogy: ". . . my father shrank into himself, and grew more and more peculiar. . . . Finally, after a severe illness, he was declared mentally unsound and removed to Melbourne. We saw him again only for a few months at the end of his life—a gentle, broken creature, who might have been a stranger."[34]

Walter Richardson was committed to Cremorne Private Asylum in Richmond, Melbourne, on September 11, 1878, and three months later was taken to the government asylum at Yarra Bend, where the asylum records show the diagnosis as "General Paralysis (incipient)."[35] Medical records and studies done on the facts of Richardson's illness by physicians, historians, and literary critics alike indicate that "general paralysis" was a term used to diagnose the majority of terminal cases of the time, especially during the late 1800s.[36] General paralysis (incipient) was correct as a diagnosis, but its most frequent source, syphilis, and the inability of medical science to detect and treat it during the early, critical stages was common.

November 19, the day after his admission to Yarra Bend, Richardson's medical report records that he "is very restless during the day and will give very indirect answers only to questions, continually humming to himself." The next day's report says: "Has had an attack of hemiplegia on the right side." And by January 25, 1879, more physical manifestations set in—ones similar to those describing Mahony's fall when he is out walking with his children in Koroit: "Another attack of paralysis today while walking about the grounds, fell and scratched his face."[37] He was released to his wife on February 24 and died on August 1, in Koroit, where Mrs. Richardson was employed as postmistress.

Henry Handel Richardson's response to her father's death is mixed: "I can't say we grieved over his death. It came rather as a relief—the same relief, in an intensified form, that we had felt during his temporary absences." She indicates, at the same time, that children "wall themselves up against unhappiness— and we were no exception to the rule." Only as an adult, when she began collecting materials for *The Fortunes of Richard Mahony*, did she "grasp at least something of what he must have suffered, both for himself and for those dependent upon him. I saw him then as a well-meaning and upright man, but so morbidly thin-skinned that he could nowhere and at no time adapt himself to his surroundings. And as such I tried to show him."[38] Recent information about his illness, already presented, indicates that while Richardson studied Hollander's *Asylum Treatment of the Insane* and several textbooks on psychiatry, she was uninterested in portraying her father as a victim of a physical disease that was simply running its course.[39] Another clue might come from this statement in her autobiography: "Here, however, I think it is only fair to add that the person who knew me best always maintained that, in my imaginary portrait of Richard Mahony, I had drawn no other than my own."[40] Medically and historically, at any rate, the record indicates that, had he not contacted cerebral syphilis, Dr. Richardson would have been a leading medical man in the history of Victoria.

III   *Preteens, Formal Schooling, and Last Years in Australia*

During her eighth and ninth year, Richardson lived with her sister and mother in a tiny, gray stone building in the western district of Victoria nearly two hundred miles from Melbourne. The town, Koroit, "consisted of a couple of banks, a hotel or two and a few dingy shops, built round the four corners of two cross-roads. We ourselves occupied one corner, the Post Office ranking next to the banks in importance; for at that time the telegraph formed the chief means of communication."[41]

Her education came from the vicarage of St. Paul's rather than the state school. She was taught general subjects by the vicar's wife, Mrs. Rupp, and encouraged in her music studies by the vicar. Her autobiography paints a rather distasteful picture of the Reverend C. L. H. Rupp, of his wife, and of the town and its residents. E. Morris Miller's careful study of the town, correspondence with its residents, and correspondence and discussions with Reverend Rupp clarify the picture with this statement: "The so-called dinginess of the place—for so it had impressed her memory, both in the novel and in *Myself When Young*—was merely a mental reaction in keeping with the despair of Mrs. Mahony in tendance on a depressed husband." Certainly, as Dorothy Green has indicated throughout *Ulysses Bound*, Richardson's identification with her mother's emotional moods was strong enough to bring about such a distortion. At this point in time, *utterly* identifying with her mother's vision, Richardson was transforming it into her childhood impressions. The possibility is also raised, since so much of the comment is simply wrong, that this section of the autobiography was written by "another hand"—perhaps Olga Roncoroni's.[42]

At this time she began composing short "poems." At Queenscliffe, after her father's death, she composed "stories" in her head while bouncing a ball against the side of the house. The stories had brought ridicule, while the "ability to rhyme love and dove and fair and hair was loudly applauded; and my productions passed from hand to hand."[43] The usual questionings about birth, reproduction, and puzzling punishments carried her quick, questioning mind through the year, together with a final visit to her father's grave at Tower Hill Cemetery, some three miles away from Koroit.[44] Her memory is that the "sight of the mound of earth stirred no emotion in me; it didn't seem to have anything to do with him. And then, I had two private worries of my own. One was the fear that my mother, who had already wiped her eyes, would demean herself by breaking down in public...."[45] The other worry, trivial in comparison, was the itch of a new crepe frock, which tormented her sensitive childhood skin. Certainly the concern for her mother is significant here in light of Richardson's distortion of Koroit in her autobiographical account.

The Richardson home in Maldon, where she lived from her tenth to sixteenth year, left quite a different impression: "In it, I spent the happiest days of my childhood, free at last of unchildish anxieties; and when, of a sleepless night, my thoughts turn homewards, it is usually in these carefree, sunlit surroundings that I find myself."[46] And it included a childhood infatuation with the young, dashing local vicar, Jack Stretch, which lingered emotionally over her entire girlhood and later life.

When she was thirteen,[47] she left home to be a boarder at the Ladies College in Melbourne (now called the Presbyterian Ladies College). An account of her school days appears in her second published novel, *The Getting of Wisdom* (1910). But the major character, Laura Rambotham, while undergoing many similar experiences, has been purposely altered in the novel to show Laura as a failure. The novel clearly intends to satirize the school experience in general as ignoring wisdom and concentrating on facts. But again, as in Richardson's picture of Koroit, it is puzzling why in her autobiography she would choose to present the same distortion. Her lack of success and her view of herself as "odd" and "unaccountable" were stressed. Also included was a condemnation of the teachers of literature and music, the routine, and the required curriculum.[48] Yet the autobiography concludes: "*The Getting of Wisdom* contained a very fair account of my doings at school, and of those I came in contact with."[49]

The facts of her years at the Ladies College are completely clear from the school records. While Richardson's 1887 diary carries the passage, "It's too much bother to live; I'm so tired of it all,"[50] everything, in fact, was quite different. During the end of her first year, she won first prizes in English and Bible, a second in history, and the second headmaster's prize for lawn tennis. In her second year, 1884, she skipped a class and won prizes in French, Latin, geometry and trigonometry, and a first in music. Her third year, when she was fifteen, included her admittance into the boarders' Literary Society—with her name on the prize lists in tennis, French, Latin, Bible, Music, Dictation, and Singing. In her fourth year she won honors in English and French and studied *seven* matriculation subjects, when only six were compulsory. But more important, she won the Senior Pianoforte Scholarship, a fact she half-remembers in her autobiography.[51] The awarding of the scholarship and Ethel Richardson's performance at the annual concert was described by the *Melbourne Age* as "the most important feature in the programme."[52] She was commended personally by the wife of the governor, encouraged to seek further study by the headmaster and the school's musical director, and praised by the famous Hungarian musician Edward Remenyi, who wrote: "You may also tell Miss Richardson that if she continues her studies under her present guidance she will not only play Hummel, but will soon enter into the inner temple of the great masters."[53] She kept the printed program her entire life, since it rests among her papers deposited at the National Library.[54] In the 1886 midyear concert one of her compositions was played with great success. This was in the presence of the critics of Melbourne's leading newspapers, who gave her space which now even an adult performer might envy.[55] Her last year at school included First Class Honors in English and history. During her years at the college, she also grew fond of a Constance Bulteel, whom she met again in London and corresponded with for the rest of her life.

When Richardson returned home, her mother had been shifted to the Melbourne post office in Swan Street—"a noisy business street [which] involved living 'over the shop,' and making do with a tiny, built-in backyard for a garden."[56] But since the Hawthorn home, still in the hands of the Richardsons, was about to be sold, Mrs. Richardson decided to resign from the postal service and travel to Europe. The motivations for such a decision are not clear. One must have been a desire to further Ethel's musical training, although the autobiography does not list it as a reason.

Nettie Palmer indicates that the 1886 Senior Pianoforte Scholarship "set her ambitious mother's mind working with schemes to take her to Europe for further training."[57] This is reinforced by Dorothy Green's more qualified statement in *Ulysses Bound* and elsewhere that it was "partly to give them [Ethel and Lilian] some first-rate musical training in the hope that they would show some aptitude for the concert platform."[58] This coincides with Kilpatrick's findings, at least on Ethel's part; the encouragement of Plumpton (her instructor) and Remenyi, together with the persuasive letter to Mrs. Richardson from the superintendent of the college, Mrs. Catherine Boys, indicates that opportunity for further study would make a concert pianist out of Ethel.[59] While such a question may seem irrelevant, it is in fact critically important to the chief facts of Richardson's life. The move to Europe and then England radically changed the course of her life. If Mrs. Richardson hadn't had what turned out to be false hopes about her daughter's musical career, the disappointment, search, and eventual shift from the musical to the literary arts would have never occurred. The exposure to Leipzig as source material, as well as the cathartic process that produced *Maurice Guest*, was crucial, not to mention the vast reading that European libraries provided. Her reading after leaving school, which included an infatuation with Longfellow's *Hiawatha* and *Hyperion*, reinforces this thesis.

IV *London and Leipzig*

Whatever the reason for going to Europe was, after a brief, unsuccessful attempt as morning governess in Toorak, Ethel left Australia with her mother and sister on August 3, 1888, on the eight-thousand-ton *Ormuz*—"the newest and finest of her line."[60] Except for a six week's visit in 1912 to check out her facts for the trilogy, she never returned to Australia.

In London, they stayed for a month with Bailey cousins and then went on to Northamptonshire to visit an aunt who was the only Bailey who had never traveled overseas. Here Richardson continued to read widely, including "a pile of mildewed novels by Bulwer Lytton, stowed away in an ancient cupboard."[61] But as most of her school experience indicates, her reading was scattered, haphazard, undisciplined, and needed the stimulus of both Leipzig and her future husband, J. G. Robertson, to provide a systematic preparation for novel writing. Ethel and her family visited Cambridge to renew acquaintances with her Irish relatives, the Henry Richardsons, who had cared for Ethel and Lilian when their parents made their grand tour of Europe in 1873. The memories she took away included a sense of the English reverence for titles, her own Irishness, an old friend's present of a copy of Macaulay's *Lays,* and an awareness as Australians that she and her sister were too talkative and independent for children. The return to Northamptonshire was followed by preparations for Leipzig, "the idea being to allow me time to settle down before entering the Conservatorium at Easter."[62] What is perhaps most interesting is Richardson's description of motive: "Life at my restless father's side had engendered [in her mother] a liking for change and movement."[63] This reading of the events that brought Richardson to Europe and her career as a novelist seems correct, since a widow, with two children, traveling to England and then to Europe with a bare four thousand pounds and no prospects sounds like Walter, not Mary. Her mother had indeed changed.

In her autobiography Leipzig is labeled "New Life."[64] It was apparently a mixture of the "happiness" she describes in the opening paragraphs and a "terror of being stared at, which became so strong it possessed her for the rest of her life."[65] The reasons for this are various and ambiguous. Some of it is a repeat of the distortion between fact and fiction in her account of the Ladies College. Her papers include both a certificate and a concert program of March 25, 1892, that testify to Richardson's accomplishments at Leipzig, as do the papers and certificates from the Presbyterian Ladies College.[66] And yet the typescript and original manuscript of *Myself When Young* emphasize in much more detail the "terror of eyes" that she felt during recitals as a pupil at the conservatory, and on page 97 of the typescript she reckons herself "a failure all around."[67] Since her fear of the concert platform and the filled recital hall appears to be immensely significant in her decision to give up music for writing,[68] it is just as important biographically as her mother's decision to leave Australia for England and Europe.

Of equal significance is her friendship, engagement, and marriage to young J. G. Robertson, a Scotsman studying for his doctorate in German literature at the University, who not only supplied her with books but "thanks to him and his suggestions, my range widened, my judgement improved."[69] The question, of course, is whether her marriage to Robertson abruptly ended a career in music or led her into writing. The autobiography states her mother's plans were "to take me back to Australia a finished pianist, there to make not only money but a name for myself."[70] But instead, Richardson's three years at Leipzig shifted from a devotion to music to an acceptance of her future husband as a cultural promoter: "Operas ranging from Flotow to Wagner, plays as far apart as Dumas and Ibsen —there was little, either old or new, that we didn't get a chance of sampling."[71]

The reactions of those who were supporting her musical career varied. Mrs. Richardson was initially opposed but finally agreed and prepared to "make the best of things." Her teachers reacted in utterly different ways, quite different from her picture of Schwartz's response to Maurice in her first novel. "Little Schreck," the autobiography indicates, "at once asked why, and, on being told, gently shook his head, but made no comment."[72] His eyes told her that women never fail to throw up a career for marriage. Weidenbach, "who always took it as a personal insult did a pupil walk out on him, naturally lost his temper."[73] Her personal estimate of Leipzig, although she had called it her "happiest years," was still the following: "there was some reason for reckoning myself a failure all around"[74]—again a suggestion of the theme of failure pervading *Maurice Guest*.

Before her marriage to Robertson in 1895, she returned rather unhappily to England with her mother and sister. After shifting residences in England for a time, they rented a house just outside the town boundary of Cambridge. Richardson admits that she "felt as much of a misfit here as I had ever been—even in Australia."[75] Here again, her feelings are transformed into Richard Mahony's attitude toward Australia when he returns to practice in England. No place carries the ultimate association of home for him. Yet with Richardson, it was the link with Leipzig and J. G. Robertson which remained constant.

V *Marriage and Her Career in Writing Begins*

Richardson's first published essay was a short expository piece entitled "Christmas in Australia," modeled directly on Lamb's essays read in her school days. This, along with a defense of Ibsen's *The Masterbuilder,* was printed in a manuscript magazine begun by one of her old shipmates aboard the *Ormuz.* After this she sent the early chapters of the translation of a Danish novel, J. P. Jacobsen's *Niels Lyhne* to the manuscript magazine. But when Robertson arrived from Germany he urged her to "work on the translation in earnest, not in play, and when it was finished we would try and find a publisher for it."[76] This was another critical step in the formation of her career in fiction: the assumption that writing was a professional enterprise worthy of one's complete attention. This critical step originated with her future husband's urging: "To be free to devote myself, day in, day out, to this dear book, and to hear what I did called serious work—the whole seemed too good to be true. However in the end N's. [J. G. Robertson's] quiet insistence prevailed."[77]

The move to a larger house in Balham, a London suburb, allowed Richardson to finish the translation of *Niels Lyhne,* undisturbed, and set her writing habits for life: ". . . I felt that I had discovered what I liked best to do. To sit alone and unobserved, behind a shut door, and play with words and ponder phrases. What a contrast to the odious publicity of the concert platform! How I could ever imagine myself fitted for it I don't know."[78] While this key statement is often quoted as proof of a pattern of isolation, withdrawal, and eventual loss of social interaction,[79] it is as well, a comprehensive statement of the motivation behind the literary drive. But for all her escape into solitude, as Kramer indicates, she would eventually face the day when the use of her life as literary material would run out: "The escapism that she practiced in her own life became the romantic core of her fiction."[80]

The translation of *Niels Lyhne* was published in 1896, the year after her marriage. Meanwhile, Robertson had completed his degree at Leipzig. Having failed in his search for a teaching appointment, he taught for six months at a girls' school, did some journalism for a short time, and then began successfully editing German texts. In order to finish Lilian's musical education, the family decided to move to Munich before Ethel's marriage. There Ethel taught English to a group of university students and had some success in writing reports on the Munich opera for English music journals. After Mrs. Richardson gave the couple three hundred pounds for their wedding present, the two decided on a wedding in Dublin and were married in midwinter, December 20, 1895, with a celebration at the home of an Australian-Irish friend. The wedding, quite an elaborate affair with two hundred guests, was written up in the *Melbourne Age*.

VI   *Munich and Strasbourg*

Returning to Munich, Robertson began contributing to a German review, *Cosmopolis*, and by the end of January, his wife was asked to translate another book from the Danish, *The Fisher Lass*, by Bjørne Bjørnson. In early May Robertson received an invitation to become lecturer at the University of Strasbourg, and the Robertsons moved to the Black Forest and the Vosges country around Strasbourg on September 25. Richardson's first attempts at original prose fiction began this year.[81] The first story is a study in themes and moods that would form central preoccupations of mind for each of her later novels. The hero—a painter afraid of losing his gift, and conscious of his limitations as an artist—encounters a figure which he interprets as Death by "the shadow of ... great world irony ... in her eyes."[82] The mood is intensely oppressive and the tone didactic as she describes a gloomy London day: "A few hungry curs slunk sullenly about, but otherwise no living creature was to be seen; human life had crept beneath cover and hidden itself away."[83] Certainly the imagery of eyes carries us back to the author's own fear of being "stared at" on the concert platform and forward to her portrayal of the eyes of Louise in *Maurice Guest* and Richard Mahony's fear of "the eyes that stare" in the trilogy. It also tends to suggest that, however happy this year might have been, Richardson was not always uplifted by her surroundings or her life. The intrusive narrator speaks again and again of "a certain grief in things as they are," of the happiness of solitude, of being "ill at ease in society"—all suggestive of the author's established moods. And like *Niels Lyhne*, much of the later part of the fragment is compressed narration—perhaps here, an unconscious imitation and at the same time a weakness of her later work. The lighter typing shows that she may, as still another alternative, have begun again at a later time, and felt rushed to go on. The second and third attempts, "Villa au Mur" and "Doctor Fraus," are even more fragmentary. "Villa au Mur" is a gothic description of a place by a worldly-wise woman and "Doctor Fraus" shows a lively, careful use of dialogue and dramatic action but remains a fragment. Certainly these early prose attempts, like most of her work, are suggestively autobiographical and as such are important to a study of her life.

Richardson's 1897 diary, recently made available for study, reveals that her first year of marriage included a heavy schedule of reading and critical writing, close and constant correspondence with her sister, frequent references to illness simply marked "bed," and now the famous first reference (September 27) to her start on *Maurice Guest*.[84] There is no direct reference to her mother's death in November, but separate notes were made that indicate the profound effect it had on her.[85] There seems to have been a mixture of guilt at not fulfilling her mother's wishes to become a concert pianist and initial disbelief that a mother of such physical strength and courage could be actually dying at the age of fifty-seven. As a result, the event points to increasing instability and fluctuation of mood in her life. And Richardson was, from her earliest years, deeply devoted to her mother and disliked her sister Lilian's power over that relationship.

This can be traced easily through the autobiography, *The Getting of Wisdom*, and her letters from her earliest years. When she writes her father a letter as a child, she unconsciously shows her jealousy: "Lilly is very fat: [I] carried a large parcel for dear mamma."[86] At age eight she writes her mother: "Lily is very homesick this evening and although it is only half past seven she is *bed* and crying she says to come down as soon as you can and write the minute you get this letter."[87] While this may seem trivial, it characterizes a relationship that later was to stimulate her interest in spiritualism—to reach a mother unreachable in life—and her portrayal of "strong" women in each of her novels: Louise and Madeline in *Maurice Guest*, Evelyn in *The Getting of Wisdom*, Mary in *The Fortunes of Richard Mahony*, and Cosima in *The Young Cosima*. The impassioned yet objective picture of the end of her mother's life, brilliant in itself, includes the following scene. Her mother is looking into a mirror:

"Do you see yourself mother," I asked.
"I see a dying woman," she said, looking into the glass with an indescribable expression on her poor haggard face.[88]

In Strasbourg she adjusted to married life and her husband's encouragement aided her writing. On Januuary 9 she sent an article on Schubert to the *Speaker*. By February 8 she was at work on "Ibsen in Translation," an attack on William Archer's translation of *John Gabriel Borkman*, published in the *Speaker*'s July 10 issue with a return letter of defense by Archer on the 24th. And she wrote an article on German women writers, which was not published.

Work to be done for the rest of the year included the Jacobsen article, later to be entitled "A Danish Poet," begun on January 13.[89] While the article expands on her admiration of Jacobsen's "romanticism imbued with the scientific spirit and essentially based on realism,"[90] it may have been partially, at least, a collaboration with her husband.[91] By the end of 1898, her reading had covered most major European and English authors, including Flaubert's works and his correspondence, Nietzsche's poems and criticism on him, George Eliot's *Life and Letters*, and general reading from Byron to Gautier.[92] Quite obviously, she was absorbing the authors that would serve as major influences on her own writing. During 1899 she read one hundred books.

The remainder of the Robertsons' stay at Strasbourg was taken up with major literary projects—Richardson's *Maurice Guest* and her husband's *History of German Literature*, marred only by an acute lung infection that left Richardson's throat permanently weak. This illness was to be rendered less painful by her sister's marriage to Otto Neustatter, and a walking tour of Switzerland. By January, 1901, specific chapter and scene progress of *Maurice Guest* is recorded through March 8, when "Maurice and Louise, End Chapters" completes the entry.[93]

The diaries during these years also reveal interests that became a part of her literary persona and her subject matter.

Her reading in George Eliot, including criticism, provided the impetus for choosing a masculine pen name, and her interest in the actress Duse led her to read *Il Fuoco*, which seems to have influenced the language of *Maurice Guest*. She also reread her parents' letters, which were now in her possession, and probably began thinking about their use in a future novel. This became her major work, *The Fortunes of Richard Mahony*. She also saw a dead baby, which later appears as the model for the Strasbourg story, "The Life and Death of Peterle Lüthy." The use of Peterle seems to carry over in the first draft of her other Strasbourg story, "The Professor's Experiment," in which the professor is called "Richard'le."[94] While her time in Strasbourg included tennis matches, walking tours in Switzerland, and bicycle tours to hear music and opera at Karlsruhe, her moods vacillated. She placed on the top of a depressing entry in her 1887 schoolgirl exercise book, "The mood of tonight, July, 1901."[95] Quite obviously, life was filled with the dark moods that provide sources for the characters of Louise, Maurice, and Mahony. And yet, the darkness of one statement is contrasted with the apparent bliss of another. A September 9, 1902, entry states: "No diary kept: because from July 22nd on I was too happy and too *unbewusst* to think about it." Yet the 1902 diary does begin on March 7 with the entry: "Tired to work; work bad." July 12 and 13 entries, as well, indicate "Not well; Bed. Long, dull day, cold and fever," and on July 17: "v. cross and tired."[96]

But the literary progress of both husband and wife continued steadily through this year. On September 13, Robertson's *History of German Literature* was published, and before the end of March, Robertson was offered the appointment to the Chair of German Literature at the University of London. By April 19 the Robertsons left for London, and by autumn were settled in a new house at 5, Lyon Road, Harrow-on-the-Hill. Robertson's notes for 1902 indicate the quickly acquired habits of withdrawal during his wife's years in London, with some of the reasons:

The house in Lyon Road was pleasant and the garden a source of pleasure. But going into London for theater or concert was strenuous as the ten minutes walk to such things in Strasbourg had never been. These unsympathetic surroundings and conditions had perhaps one good result: that in Harrow Henry buried herself as never before in her book. . . . she felt spiritually isolated. Also she found no congenial friends in music. Thus her life became, unfortunately, more solitary, and the "living alone" only increased with the years.[97]

The later move to 90 Regents Park Road was of little help; from this year until her husband's death in 1933, she found London more and more congenial as a place to absorb herself in the inward writing experience.

VII *London and the Publication of* Maurice Guest

In "Some Notes on My Books," Henry Handel Richardson says that "my first plan [for *Maurice Guest*] had been hardly more than that of pinning the happy Leipzig days to paper. But other forces were at work; and very soon the characters involved in the tragic love story had it their own way."[98] This book, as all that were to follow, included much of her inner personality of fluctuating moods. Before it was published in August, 1908, William Heinemann asked that the book be reduced twenty thousand words, with the admission from the author that "my present regret is that I did not do the job [the cutting] still more thoroughly. . . ."[99] Manuscript studies of her method of revision reveal that while the book was an extraordinary first novel, her methods of revision are not clear yet. Characteristic were cuts in adjectives, clichés, revision of diction, and elimination of authorial intrusions and yet side by side with each of these omissions were left passages of superfluous verbiage.[100] I suspect these are the revisions she regrets not completing, and this remark is repeated when she was asked to prepare the American edition of *Maurice Guest* in 1930.

The reviews of *Maurice Guest* varied a great deal, from "Morbid, depressing, dull, verbose, degraded, coarse, erotic, and neurotic" to "the Best Novel of the Last Five Years."[101] William Heinemann's own comments indicate the strength of his belief in the book, included later in detail in his autobiography and his private comments to Richardson: "Remember . . . whatever happens, I shall never regret having published *Maurice*

Guest."[102] The most penetrating compliment was Somerset Maugham's comment that it was a great novel "in the way the novels of Tolstoi are great" and that it had considerable influence on writers of the time.[103] This widespread influence can be verified in a number of later imitations and Richardson's own comment: "... the passionate shades of Maurice and Louise rose again in many a novel of that time: and I had to see A and B and C win the laurels denied to me."[104] Even more revealing are her husband's notes for a never to be completed critical book on her: "To the student of immediately pre-war days, following the somewhat depressing stiffening on doctrinaire lives of Flaubert's great art in the books of the later generation, Henry Handel Richardson's *Maurice Guest*, with its appealing psychological realism, was a revelation not to be forgotten."[105]

Robertson's published essay, "The Art of Henry Handel Richardson," expands on this statement: "[*Maurice Guest*] stands in its essentials nearer to the peculiarly Slavonic and Germanic development of realism. . . . From Flaubert Henry Handel Richardson may have learned her best lessons in the art and technique of presenting her matter, but the master that stands behind the most impressive pages of her work is unquestionably Dostoevsky."[106] The range of the above comments show the fruits of her reading in Strasbourg, the extraordinary quality of her first novel, and from the beginning, her husband's supportive role as appreciative critic, general source of encouragement, and later, supplier of source materials from the British Museum.

VIII   The Getting of Wisdom

In 1910 her second novel, *The Getting of Wisdom*, was published. Begun while she was working on *Maurice Guest*, "partly as a relief from that book's growing gloom, partly to fill the hours of a wet summer in the Bavarian mountains,"[107] this book was her personal favorite because it was "a 'light spot' between *Maurice Guest*, short, written with ease, treated a time of happy memories, but was not taken ironically, as it was intended."[108] In "Some Notes on My Books" she says:

I can recall only three who laughed as they were meant to: William Heinemann, Edmund Gosse, H. G. Wells. For the rest the book was born and died, both here and in America, in the autumn of 1910; and it lay like a corpse within its grave until, in 1924, I rubbed my eyes to see Gerald Gould refer to it as "the best of all contemporary school stories."[109]

The direction of her writing career was now set. While great in themselves, *Maurice Guest* and *The Getting of Wisdom* represent the author's apprenticeship to her art. The trilogy, her next work, shows her confident in the art and the form of the realist. While, by her own admission and the consensus of critics, she applied her principles of objective observation to life in London, her life in London from 1903 until her husband's death in 1933 was the life of her writing. And yet she obtained a seat at the Old Bailey to hear the murder trials, she went to boxing matches in South London, where the fights were so gruesome her male escort "had to go out for a time because the sight of blood made him feel sick,"[110] and she asked to be escorted to places in Limehouse frequented by opium smokers. She studied the written records of the dreams of her secretary, Olga Roncoroni, who was undergoing psychoanalysis at the first psychoanalytic clinic in England using the Freudian method of analysis. She joined three psychic research societies in London, and in the course of forty years she sat with the best-known mediums of the day.

IX   *The Writing and Publication of the Trilogy*

Sometime before 1912 Richardson began *Australia Felix*. Her first work involved the compilation of four volumes of notes, comprising 342 pages, complete with index, based on extensive reading in the histories of the period, supplied to her by her husband. These were principally Thomas M'Combie's *Australian Sketches,* William Howitt's *Land, Labour and Gold; or Two Years in Victoria,* and William Kelly's *Life in Victoria.*[111] After completing the notes, she checked or underlined sections dealing with mining, scenery, and vegetation, and the clothes, speech, and manners of the miners. After completing much of the first draft of *Australia Felix,* she journeyed to Australia with her husband late in 1912 to check her facts. Her 1912 diary notes the objectivity with which she pursued her checking of facts as she developed detachment from Mahony's vision of Australia. For example, during the journey from Melbourne to Geelong by rail can be seen "when wet, an unbearably *sad* landscape in colour."[112] In Ballarat, she notes her father's former home as 'House numbered 4 Webster St.";[113] and in Melbourne she notes "easy familiarity of people as long as one is well and *young*, and in good spirits, but there are times when it grates horribly, and must end by maddening."[114] All these are positions a sensitive, rather stuffy young man would take toward his environment, and, as the critic Leonie Kramer remarks, are an essentially Anglo-Australian vision of the country that *both* the fictional Mahony and its author would share.[115] Richard Mahony, then, is a more accurate psychological vision of her Australia.

While *Australia Felix* was completed in 1915, it was not published until 1917, when William Heinemann felt England had adjusted to "a state of war: 'business as usual' was the slogan."[116] The book had reasonably good sales in England and America but was so unknown in Richardson's native Australia that reviews the author remembers best range from "a dull but honest volume" to "might have been written by a retired grocer."[117]

Because of the war, chronic ill-health, forced removal from her home, the loss of a trusted secretary, and a difficult psychological adjustment from Germany's earlier role in her life as the center of culture, learning, and music, the second volume of the trilogy, *The Way Home*, was not begun until 1919. Between 1915 and that time, with her mind only on the early fruitful days in Leipzig, she wrote two somber stories about the city, "The Life and Death of Peterle Lüthy" and "The Professor's Experiment," later collected in *The End of a Childhood*. Her nephew, Walter Lindesay Neustatter, presents a detached, positive picture of her to counteract these depressive periods by characterizing her as "an artist at heart."[118]

During the incessant air raids of the winter of 1917–18, her doctor ordered her away from London to the Robertsons' retreat at Dorset House in Lyme Regis, Dorset, on Lyme Bay in south-

western England. When she returned to London, further inter-
ruptions—taking a friend, Olga Roncoroni, to a clinic five days a
week for Freudian treatment—prevented the appearance of *The
Way Home* until 1925. But with the death of William Heinemann in 1921 her chief source of support within the publishing
world was lost. The book barely sold a thousand copies and so
depressed her that she despaired "of the use and the sense of
going on with Mahony's story."[119] The only favorable reviews
came, ironically, from Germany and Sweden.

But she went on. Nettie Palmer's comments upon first meeting
Richardson were that she had a detached but determined nature,
a steady power of concentration, and a passionate interest in
human relationships and character.[120] A 1927 letter to Palmer
indicates how determined she was to finish the trilogy regardless
of its reception and to make it valuable to later generations of
Australian readers:

I needn't say how much I value an Australian audience. . . . Volume
III will not be different from its predecessors. It was left to the next
generation to feel at "home," to love its light and spaciousness; much
else besides—whether I shall go on with their fortunes I can't say.
It will depend in part on the reception given to the present war
as a whole.[121]

Her husband's part in the last volume was twofold. In *Australia Felix* and *The Way Home,* it had been a steady supply
of research materials and emotional support—but never urging
or suggesting—of her tragic realist stance toward the character
of Richard Mahony. Since the early 1920s he had been lecturing
and writing at the University of London on the value of dispas-
sionate objectivity in Dostoevski, Tolstoy, Stendhal, and even
the nineteenth-century Danish novelist Henrik Pontoppidan. In
his manuscript notes on Richard Mahony, he defends the artistic
value and yet admits to the commercial unpopularity of fictional
truth. While Walter Richardson's insanity and death correspond
to the death of Richard Mahony, her sorting out of fact and
fiction place the trilogy in the sphere of detached, objective,
and great realistic art.[122] Added to this can be Professor Manning
Clarke's comment that Richardson went through a specific

psychic change between writing *The Way Home* and *Ultima Thule,* which intuitively deepened her conception of tragic realism. He suggested that this change was due to the war itself.[123] Certainly her disillusionment over the German invasion of Europe in this war (and the next) compelled her to a tragic feeling of being cut off from a symbolic home. This led her, perhaps, to think of Australia as the tragically "lost" home it became to Mahony.

In any event, *Ultima Thule* was painstakingly completed during the summer of 1928, but it was refused publication by Heinemann because sales on *The Way Home* had been minimal. Her husband settled the matter by bearing the cost of an edition of one thousand copies, and the book appeared, as she says, "unheralded, unpuffed" on January 9, 1929, at the author's expense.[124] As both the author and Arnold Gyde indicate, Gerald Gould's penetrating review in the following Sunday's *Observer* made the book an immediate success; *Ultima Thule* was reprinted the next week by Heinemann with new impressions in February, March, May, and June. The costs of the first printing were refunded the Robertsons. Published by Norton the same year in the United States, it became a book-club choice with eighty thousand copies sold the first month.[125] In 1930, Heinemann published the trilogy in one volume. By 1940 it had been reprinted five times in the one-volume collected edition, and revised editions of *The Getting of Wisdom* and *Maurice Guest* appeared. Her success was complete. For her work, she won the Australian Gold Medal for Literature and later the King George Jubilee medal. Her writing was well known in Australia, America, England, and on the Continent by the midthirties.

X *Her Husband's Death and the Move to Green Ridges, Sussex*

While much of Richardson's secluded life in London still remains an accounting of books written rather than of relationships and events, the death of her husband in 1933 shattered her writing life almost completely. As Green says, "her husband had in effect taken over the role of both parents; and she had been all her life groping for a sign from both parents, not fixated on one of them. . . ."[126] "There seems little doubt that, in Robertson, Richardson found educator, father, mother, husband, and psychiatrist."[127] And most critics and scholars of Richardson agree that her husband provided ideal surroundings for her writing for over twenty years, even to the particulars of leaving sharpened pencils on her writing desk each morning.

The loss of such a foothold obviously took on the character of a double death. But even Robertson's selflessness transcended his physical death to prevent his wife's inability to cope with such a loss. As Olga Roncoroni said, he made a specific request of her and extracted a weighty promise to take care of his wife until *her* death. Roncoroni's further comment, during my interview with her on March 27, 1974, was that she *never* took that promise lightly. Its demands became her life's preoccupation— in fact drained that life.[128] Shouldering the role of father, mother, husband, and psychiatrist must have been insurmountable for a woman who herself had had years of psychiatric treatment, had been withdrawn since a child, and while much younger than Richardson, suffered physical as well as mental ailments. How both lives continued out of mental hospitals is somewhat of a miracle. Immediately after Richardson's death in 1946, Roncoroni found herself unable to cope and voluntarily admitted herself to a hospital for care.

Richardson's writing life was in total disorder. As early as 1931 she had begun collecting research books, with her husband's help, for her last novel, *The Young Cosima*. This stopped, of course, and the move to Green Ridges set the house in a state of upheaval. The vastness of the Wagnerian subject also began to overwhelm her. In 1931 she had consented to the publication by Ulysses Press of London of a slim volume of short stories, which included "Death," retitled "Mary Christiana," and "The Life and Death of Peterle Lüthy." The volume was favorably reviewed, in particular by T. H. Lawrence.[129] Its theme was death. "Mary Christina" was drawn originally from her notes on her mother's death in 1897. Reconsideration of a story about the most momentous loss of her early life must surely have affected her later thoughts about her husband's death.

In 1934 she also consented to the publication of a collection of her short stories, *The End of a Childhood*. While the book

was indifferently reviewed, Green speculates that the "second"
death of her mother described in the four chapters of the title
story suggest her feeling of withdrawal at the death of Robertson. In those chapters Cuffy continually asks the question, "When
Mother went out, would she ever come back?" The answer in
adult life, at this critical point, seems to be clearly no.

XI   The Young Cosima *and Final Years at Green Ridges*

The publication of *The Young Cosima* in 1939, after a great
deal of difficulty, ends her career in fiction. The unfinished autobiography was published posthumously in 1948. Four chapters of
a novel on London low life, entitled *Nick and Sanny*, were
destroyed on the author's instructions by Olga Roncoroni.[130]
While Miss Roncoroni read the chapters and felt them a strong
study of interrelationship in a realistic London setting, she
would reveal no more than that during her interview with me.[131]

Since Miss Roncoroni was Richardson's personal secretary and
typist during this part of her life, she was particularly involved
in the writer's last efforts. Her attempts to organize Richardson's
collection of over fifty books on Wagner for the author's work
illustrated her attempt to fulfill Robertson's role as scholar and
supplier of research materials. Her anger, as well, at the poor
reception of the book, developed the role of promoter and de-
fender. Yet critics ranging from the usually sympathetic, such as
Nettie Palmer, to Leonie Kramer, who was usually objective but
critical, support the statement that "it could have been written
by anyone with patience and industry." The style was hardly
recognizable as that of the author of *Maurice Guest* or *Richard
Mahony.*[132]

And finally Roncoroni had to take on the role of "counter-
attacking" critic, since a case could easily be made for Wagner's
antisemitic attitudes and the outbreak of World War II as the
prime reasons for its poor reception. And indeed war was upon
them, increasing Olga's domestic work load and still another
role—this time as surrogate mother. Conditions described a year
earlier in a letter to Miss Kathleen Ussher indicate the terrors
of "bomb alley." They seem to be strangely commonplace to a
woman filled with psychological disturbances: "We are never

free from alerts, bells, alarms and expansions of various kinds. One never knows what will happen next."[133] V-E Day in Richardson's diary is simply marked with the words themselves surrounded by a red circle. Then "too war-worn to make anything of it."[134]

On March 30, 1946, Henry Handel Richardson died at Green Ridges. She had survived the war almost determined to yield her last physical and mental strength to endure a world crisis. And yet her writing career stopped. As early as April, 1941, she wrote in her notebook: "For all she was hailed as a great innovator, Virginia Woolf's roots were in the 'nineties.' Her forebearers were the aesthetes, Yellow-Bookists, Arthur Symons and poets of 'the vial and the vine.' And above all Pater. Much of her fine writing comes direct from him."[135] She disliked "phrase-making" and was critical of the literary style of Patrick White, because it drew attention to itself.[136] From Woolf to White, then, she remained a realist, literally out of the mainstream of the art of the novel of her time. While she was nominated for a Nobel Prize in 1932, it was left to the "phrase-maker" Patrick White to win it in 1973 and to Woolf to gain immortality as one of the great experimentalists of English literature. Richardson remained, to the last, a great realist both in and out of her time.

CHAPTER 2

Henry Handel Richardson as a Translator

I Niels Lyhne

HENRY Handel Richardson began her career in fiction as a translator of two novels, *Niels Lyhne* (1898),[1] by J. P. Jacobsen, and *The Fisher Lass* (1898),[2] by Björnstjerne Björnson. This came after two short articles, "Christmas in Australia,"[3] an ordinary piece for a British audience, and the second, a defense of Ibsen's *The Masterbuilder*[4] for the same amateur magazine. While much of her work on the translations shows a meticulous, careful working out of the methods of an emerging realist, the thematic influence these works had on her later fiction is perhaps more valuable than her skill as a translator.

Born in Denmark in the early nineteenth century, Niels Lyhne is portrayed as the son of a mediocre landed gentleman and a mother who "kept alive her romantic spirit in rather humdrum, prosaic surroundings, and who instilled into her son's mind from childhood the idea that he was to be a poet."[5] At twelve Niels becomes infatuated with a visitor, Edele, a twenty-six-year-old aunt who rejects his offer of flowers as she in turn cruelly rejects the love of the village tutor, Herr Bigum. Edele dies, despite Niels's passionate prayers to God to save her life, and the result is his break with God. He goes to Copenhagen as a student, where he meets and courts Fru Boye, a sophisticated coquette, but after a lengthy relationship she dismisses him. His father's death is followed by a trip to alpine Switzerland, where he tends his ailing mother. But the natural beauty fails to either fulfill her dreams or keep her from death.

Niels's religious and emotional crises culminate in a long

poetic dialogue with an atheist, Dr. Hjerrild, on the future of man without God, and on the difficulties of the inspired re-evaluation of existence that will take place. He prepares without success for his poetic vocation. Erik Refstrup, a friend and painter whose inspiration and marriage are flagging next demands his attention.

Erik's wife, Fennimore, an old friend, and Niels, become lovers but separate when Erik's death after a drunken bout fills Fennimore with rage and guilt. Niels returns to his ancestral estate, occupies himself with farming, and eventually marries a young neighbor girl, Greta, who seems to accept his love and his religion more than the others of his life. Ironically, she dies, but before her death she renounces her atheism. Soon after, their son dies, despite Niels's decision to pray to God. Spiritually lost, Niels joins the army, goes off to war, and during a battle is fatally wounded in the chest. Rejecting religion once more, he dies unresolved in spirit. Richardson writes in *Myself When Young*, "This book, J. P. Jacobsen's *Niels Lyhne*, one of those sent by N. [J. G. Robertson], had stirred me as few books have ever done either before or since, and I was green enough to imagine that others would be equally impressed."[6] In her "Preface" to *Niels Lyhne*, she stresses that "in it he [Jacobsen] opened up for his contemporaries a new world, a romanticism that was free from the mystic and unconscious element of the older school that centered in *Dehlenschläger*, a romanticism imbued with the scientific spirit and essentially based on realism."[7]

Both comments indicate a depth of feeling and absorption that can be easily traced through parallels between the character of Niels and Maurice, and between Laura in *The Getting of Wisdom* and Petra in *The Fisher Lass*. Her major characters seem to be conceived as romantics in an intensely realistic world. In her study of Jacobsen, "A Danish Poet," published in 1897, she indicates that Jacobsen writes with the "exceeding delicacy of feeling" of "a mental aristocrat," who although a devotee of Flaubert, "wore Naturalism only as an outer garment" and was by temperament more closely akin "to the old Romantic novelists and the new psychological novelists."[8] This is just as revealing, for two reasons: first, it fits into the most recent critical discoveries about the relationship between Richardson's life—her psyche—and her art;[9] second, it shows that Richardson's naturalistic and realistic tools, as she meant them to be used, were not her enslavement but her means to shape and reshape a long work of fiction.

Niels Lyhne first appeared in 1880, the second and last novel of Jens Peter Jacobsen. Dorothy Green observes that the translation was not only Richardson's first professional task, but gave her the symbol that was to later "serve for her work as a whole . . . the subtitle of the work *Siren Voices*."[10] The name is taken from a remark made by Jacobsen in describing the novel: for him the "siren voices" were the voices of tradition and of childhood memories and the condemning thunder of society all raised in unison to deter the freethinker from remaining faithful to atheism. Jacobsen had set out to write a book about freethinkers.[11]

The siren voices, as voices of convention, tradition, and anger at the freethinker, are resisted by Laura as a child; Schilsky, Louise, and Krafft as young adults; Richard Mahony, in the trilogy; and Cosima and Wagner in Richardson's last novel. In Jacobsen's novel, the instance of atheism is central, but in Richardson it is simply the strength to resist, as Ulysses resisted the sirens' song by being lashed to the mast of his ship. Niels Lyhne gives up his faith, and, when he finally marries, he converts his wife to atheism. His only lapse into "convention" comes in moments of utter despair, and, like Richardson's heroes, he returns to even a higher atheism: "For the new ideal, Atheism, the holy cause of truth—what was the aim of it all, what *was* it all in fact, but a tinsel-name for the simple endeavours to bear life as it was . . . and let it take shape according to the laws that govern it."[12]

Shocked by the death of his wife and child, Niels enlists in the army, is wounded, and refusing the consolations of faith, dies the harsh death of a skeptic. Dorothy Green points to two key conversations in the book that indicate both Jacobsen's position and Richardson's use of it: the conversation between Niels and his friend Hjerrild on the strengths and weaknesses of atheism, and a similar conversation at Niels's deathbed.[13] The first results in Hjerrild's observation that "you must have wonderful faith in humanity. Why, atheism will end by making greater demands on it than Christianity does."[14] In the second Hjerrild comments that "if I were God I would rather save the one who did not turn round at the last moment."[15] Both remarks sum up Jacobsen's and, in turn, Richardson's determination to portray their central characters as spirits contained in a kind of bondage by the conventions of the world. And for Green, they also sum up Richardson's personality as a total being of self-defense against the world, bound "to the mast of her own work."[16] Richardson's 1941 notebook, like her letters to her publisher Heinemann late in her life, reveal the extent to which she bound herself to her work. She envisioned a harsh world outside her study door, edged with recrimination and hatred, which is expressed her 1941 notebook:

> Had I been taken up at the time of *Maurice Guest,* everything might have turned out differently for me. I was quite ready then to be sociable. But the long, hard years of neglect did their work, and by 1929 I had lost all desire to come out of my shell.
>
> Perhaps it was better so. My mind is easily dissipated, and any gain in experience might have been counter balanced by a loss of the one-sidedness needed for a really long look.[17]

Her letter of September 13, 1944, to Captain Gyde, in possession of Heinemann in the Richardson file, indicates an even later admission: "You ask if I mind being forgotten. I suppose I do, at heart. But I don't brood on it, I'm used to it."[18] Since "being used to it," in the metaphor of "Ulysses Bound," is presumably being tied to a mast to resist society's siren voices, *Niels Lyhne* also acted as a catalyst to produce two conflicting archetypal characters of the self and the creative self—the settler and the nomad, "the soul which could not decide between shadow and substance, the divided mind seeking wholeness."[19]

Since *Maurice Guest* was her first novel, much of her creative self was transferred from book to book, as the roles switched from translator to creative writer. Herr Bigum, Niels's tutor, for example, is similar to Maurice himself. Both are obsessively in love with unobtainable women; and both women in turn are in love with great artists. Obsessive love in Fennimore, for Niels's brother Erik, parallels Louise's passion over Schilsky in

Maurice Guest. And certainly Niels's sense of the impermanence of human joy fills Maurice's consciousness after Schilsky comes to take Louise away. Green's analysis of other parallels suggests that Richardson found similarities between her life experience and the romantic hero of Jacobsen's novel which were later metamorphosed into a literary aesthetic. Green argues persuasively that the concepts of the settler and the nomad, the impermanence of human existence, and the divided self found in *Niels Lyhne* can be traced through *The Getting of Wisdom,* the trilogy, and even *The Young Cosima.*[20]

While Richardson's literary aesthetic was certainly shaped by a combination of her reading, her job as a translator, and her life experience, it is helpful but not entirely relevant to see specific parallels between the characters in a novelist's entire gallery and those in an early book she translated. Artistic metamorphosis, by all means, took place, but did not Richardson also expand, alter, and mature her literary aesthetic and grow with each novel? Some clues as to her methods while translating *Niels Lyhne* might suggest an early, major step in this process of growth. Certainly she discovered an art form that suited her personality, and this came after a period of indecision:

For my work on *Niels* continued to absorb me, and I felt that at last I had discovered what I liked best to do. To sit alone and unobserved, behind a shut door, and play with words and ponder phrases. (What a contrast to the odious publicity of the concert-platform! How could ever I imagine myself fitted for it I didn't know.)[21]

At the same time that her work on Jacobsen's book had served as the impetus for a career, translation also initiated a realist's concern for accuracy of detail. Her admiration for Ibsen's plays resulted in a critical attack on William Archer's translation of Ibsen's *John Gabriel Borkman,*[22] which she wrote while she was translating *Niels Lyhne.* The attack concerns Archer's linguistic inaccuracies, his failure to reproduce idomatic equivalents, his own poor English style, his failure to preserve Ibsen's prose style, and finally his general ability to produce a work of literature. And over the years that her own work was being translated, Richardson comments upon the poor quality of the work.

In "Some Notes on My Books," she complains of a *Maurice
Guest* translation: "In 1912 Fischer of Berlin brought it out
at a prohibitive price and in a particularly wooden translation."[23]
And in a letter of September 30, 1930, to Nettie Palmer, she says:

> You ask me if I was satisfied with the German translation of *Maurice
> Guest*. At the time I was; now I am not so sure; and I always thought
> it a pity that its excessive length had to be added to. But it is very
> difficult to say a thing *briefly* in German. That is why Nietzsche was
> of such infinite value to German literature. His style compares with
> the best in any language and shows that German does not *need* to
> be ponderous and long-winded.[24]

Dymphna Clark, in "The Aurora Borealis: Henry Handel
Richardson as a Translator," the most recent and thorough study
of Henry Handel Richardson as a translator, notes that, "as for
accuracy, no translator could have been more conscientious.
Everywhere there is evidence of a painstaking determination to
leave nothing out—or almost nothing."[25] As a translator, then,
Richardson both acquired and applied the principles of the
realist to her first full-length work: the careful and complete
accumulation of word, phrase, idiom, and sentence to yield the
most faithful transcription of the author's intent. "Scarcely one
of Jacobsen's matted knots of epithets and abstractions," Clark
goes on, "is glossed over in her English text."[26]

But along with this thoroughness come some of the problems
basic to the realist and the translator. Does thoroughness most
often yield the best equivalent? Clark's conclusions seem to be
the following: (1) in the translation of abstract passages that
convey Jacobsen's prose-poetry of ideas, and the intricacies of his
style, Richardson's abilities faltered; and (2) in the translation
of strong emotional or narrative passages, including the poetic
passage from Oehlenschlager's *Helge*, she is superior. Richardson's difficulties were those of the realistic method itself—difficulties that she faced again in the years when she was writing her
greatest novels. As Clark contends,

> what lays the most deadening hand of all on much of this transla-
> tion is Henry Handel Richardson's common habit of translating
> troublesome passages if not word for word then phrase by phrase in
> schooldesk style. Fidelity to the original literal meaning may be

achieved in this way, but it leaves no chance of recapturing the melody of rhythm of the original—or indeed of achieving a version with a rhythm and melody of its own, which is usually the best that can be hoped for.[27]

Free translation, however critical she is of it in Archer's version of *John Gabriel Borkman*, seems to be her strength, rare as it may be. And by contrast, Jacobsen's rich, sensuousness of style—including passages that show wit, irony, and a tendency to apostrophize after a lengthy rhetorical or intensely emotional paragraph—is more often lost than preserved.[28] But there are times when Richardson skillfully translates the aphorisms, a key to her style.

The conclusions for Richardson's art again seem obvious: emotional involvement and a rapidly developing skill for dramatic narration brought out her genius; abstractness of prose and a sustained intricacy of stylistic subtlety brought out her weakness. Two statements immediately come to mind, by two critics who have spent a considerable amount of time studying Richardson: (1) she is a writer of the emotions;[29] and (2) she is not a "natural" writer.[30] Certainly Dorothy Green's *Ulysses Bound* is a testament to the inseparable bond between Richardson's emotional life and her work, and the manuscript drafts in the Australian National Library in Canberra testify to the fact that writing and rewriting was a painful, carefully developing process for her. Even the final manuscript versions from which each of the books was printed show stylistic revision.[31] Characteristic revisions, for example, in the final copy of *Maurice Guest* include adjectival deletions: "His walk brought him to a broad [and rapid] stream"[32]; shifts in diction "His choice had fallen on Stuttgart: it was far away [deleted for 'distant'] from Leipzig"[33]; and deletion of authorial intrusions.[34]

In Henry Handel Richardson's translation of *Niels Lyhne*, Clark sums up these early stylistic difficulties: (1) a hesitation to retain the word order of the original, even when it is acceptable in English; (2) a failure to reproduce Jacobsen's "stylistic trick of repeating—sometimes in a variant—the same word or root-word"; and (3) a failure often "to give the pithy quality of the original."[35]

Richardson's work as a translator of *Niels Lyhne,* then, profoundly shaped her method as a realist and provided her with autobiographical analogues which in turn inspired character, plot, and tone in *Maurice Guest* and in the novels that followed. While Richardson herself states she "soaked herself" in French, Russian, German, and Scandinavian literature"; mastered "how a theme was to be handled objectively" from Flaubert; and found herself influenced by the great Russians, Tolstoy and Dostoevski, in *Maurice Guest,*[36] it is clear that she was just as profoundly influenced by Jacobsen as she wrote this first novel. In "Some Notes on My Books," she mentions the Leipzig years of preparatory reading of Russian, French, Danish, and Norwegian books, "in those admirable translations for which the Germany of that time was famous."[37]

J. G. Robertson's essay "The Art of Henry Handel Richardson" seems to illustrate that *Maurice Guest* was influenced by a number of sources, and, contrary to Henry Handel Richardson's statement of Russian influences, it implies—as do other Richardson scholars—that Scandinavian influences were important. The Scandinavian influence is often associated with the effect her translation of Björnson's *Fiskerjenten* had on her second novel, *The Getting of Wisdom.*[38]

But while influences can be pointed out in *Fiskerjenten,* *Maurice Guest* comes closer to a combination of the Slavonic, Germanic, *and* Scandinavian conception of realism than the Russian or French one. Her Zolaesque methods of writing *Australia Felix* are accurate, but those she used in writing *Maurice Guest* are not.[39] Green attributes it to a complex interaction of psychological motives:

... to distract attention from what might be construed as personal material in the novel. To claim it was "original" would be to stress its personal quality. To indicate certain sources rather than others would provide evidence of where the writer's personal interests lay. To emphasize others less personal is the only recourse possible.[40]

CHAPTER 3

Maurice Guest

I Summary

*M**aurice Guest* (1908), Henry Handel Richardson's first novel,
outlines the life of a young Englishman from a provincial
village who arrives in Leipzig to study piano against his parents' wishes. He quickly meets Madeline Wade, a self-sufficient
English girl who guides him to the best instructor, Schwartz.
Schwartz informs Maurice that with time he "will undertake to
make something"[1] of him. Unfortunately, rather than devoting
himself to the piano, Guest falls in love with Louise Dufrayer,
a young Australian girl studying in the same city. Louise responds
indifferently, since she is passionately in love with the conservatory's young genius, Schilsky. While Maurice pursues her, she
simply uses his infatuation as a counterbalance against Schilsky's
sporadic rejections of her. After months of devotion to her,
Maurice carries her through an illness brought on by Schilsky's
departure from Leipzig and his irresponsible, destructive affair
with an American girl, Ephie Cayhill. Just as love seems to be
an unrewarding, tragic obsession for Maurice, Louise agrees
to a three-week idyll in Rochlitz. When Schilsky returns, Maurice
stupidly tells Louise and realizes too late that he has not only
lost his career over her but his love, for Schilsky's superior
musical genius draws Louise back to him, and they are married.
Maurice fails to compromise his lesser talents in love and music.
He commits suicide at the spot where he first met Louise
Dufrayer. The book ends with a description of Schilsky's later
success amid gossip over the infamous Louise, a woman "an
English chap shot himself"[2] over. The final statement on Schilsky, music, and fame sums up Richardson's intent: "His new
symphonic poem, *Uber die letzten Dinge*, had drawn down on

his head that mixture of extravagant laudation and abusive derision, which constitutes fame."[3]

At the same time, as Dorothy Green notes, the novel's conclusion leaves Louise's lasting happiness in doubt. It does *not* demonstrate, as the typical Victorian novel of the period would, the rounding off of character, but a "cry of protest against the fundamental irrationality at the heart of things."[4]

II *Literary Analysis*

Maurice Guest has been described as a "great love story,"[5] an "analysis of the nature of genius,"[6] and "a tragedy of two people who are musicians."[7] It has also been described as a novel that first introduces Richardson's application of a "romanticism imbued with the scientific spirit, and essentially based on realism."[8] It is all of these things. Certainly, it is a somber novel of scientific realism, which develops romantic central characters, a neutral narrator, and Henry Handel Richardson's continuing concern with the theme of failure.

The world of *Maurice Guest,* as in all her novels, is inhabited by two kinds of people: those who "live and abide by the ordinary standards of life" and those who "legislate for themselves."[9] The failure, Maurice, has aspirations beyond his talents. The successes, Schilsky, Krafft, and Louise Dufrayer, are the Nietzschean *Ubermenschen* who order their lives beyond moral and social responsibility. Louise rejects marriage, because she asserts a life of permanent, ideal passion without its responsibilities. Schilsky and Krafft assert their talent in a sphere of personal relationships. And Maurice, a victim of obsessive love, is temperamentally incapable of meeting the demands of musical life. The central conflict of the novel becomes the clash between Maurice and Louise, who reject the demands of the real world. Louise's passion consumes her, but it is made perfect in the real world. She has successfully fused her insular, self-sufficient ideal of passion without responsibility by making others instruments of her own fulfillment as a "romantic introvert." Maurice, on the other hand, has turned from blind passion to a distortion of values that ends in hatred, recrimination, insane jealousy, suspicion, and finally suicide. Guest is an essentially ordinary young man caught up in the undemocratic class of the artist, a class that treats him indifferently and takes its own extraordinary rights and privileges. But artistic genius and a "genius for love" are never contradictory in Leipzig; instead, they are complementary. Louise, like Salli in Richardson's short story, "Succedaneum," fulfills her role as a lover of artists. Jerome, in that story, and Schilsky in *Maurice Guest*, are examples of Nietzschean artists who need their Sallis and their Louises when their creative self stops. In fact, they become "advanced nihilists"—amoral, destructive, possessed by death, fascinated by an absorption into nothingness. When Jerome decides to tear up the letter of reconciliation to Salli and send a telegram instead that says: "*Am Not Coming Back. Return home*," we know he is a Schilsky, driven on by a demonlike power, making his own rules, and flaunting the conventions of ordinary life. The world of art is an indifferent world, sometimes responsive, often hostile, but those who rest in the center rarely see it.

Madeline seems to be both a seer and yet, like Maurice, a quite ordinary talent. Like Dove, she is a conformist and career oriented. Her good sense saves her, however. It allows her the clarity and detachment of perception through which the reader can decide who is normal in Leipzig and who is not. She is a controlling sensibility for the novel's neutral narrator. When she calls Schilsky amoral, we know Madeline to be mouthing the sentiments of a conventional moralist, and yet, for Maurice, and perhaps for the world, they are the saving conventionalities. Maurice is an anguished romantic because he fails to see the limits to his artistic and emotional world; he has, in other words, neglected to admit the foolishness of his love even after Madeline reminds him again and again of Louise's aimless, chaotic life. Maurice confronts Louise's craving for an ideal love with his own destructive, naive passion. He has come to her with specific alternatives in mind. Maurice comes to Leipzig with his father's early ambition: "to escape from harsh reality into the mollifying atmosphere of music." But he is quite aware of his father's compromise of turning "his back on his visions haunting his youth."[10] He senses for a moment or two the foolishness of persisting, and yet remains horrifyingly romantic and a self-destructive failure.

Maurice Guest is the history of a young English provincial
who *aspires* to be a musician. He travels to Leipzig to study but
then fails in both love and art and commits suicide. We are led
to believe he fails because he lacks both the talent and temperament for a life of artistry. The book opens with Maurice's
arrival in Leipzig, which becomes an exploration into the physical and emotional dimensions of a musical initiate. He has just
emerged from the new *Gewandhaus* after being intoxicated by
the music of a skillful "lank-haired Belgian violinist." He follows
the crowd to the nearby woods, which provides "a fresh impulse
to life; ... under the sway of a twofold intoxication: great music
and a great day rich in promise."[11] Having arrived in Leipzig
that very day, he fuses the performance with his dreamy, idyllic
view of himself as a famous, disciplined artist; and Maurice
ironically promises himself that "no other fancy or interest should
share his heart with it."[12] He sees the town, as well, through an
ultraromantic vision of "the renowned figures that had once"[13]
walked these streets. This is to be contrasted to the commercial streets of Leipzig in the present; and Richardson reminds
us: "as is usual with active-brained dreamers, he had little or
no eye for the real life about him."[14] This, as well, is ironic,
since a realistic existence of love and living eludes Maurice
from the beginning. Even when he meets the practical-minded
Madeline and discovers that the violinist's performance was a
"dull aria ... and indifferently played symphony ... not a fresh
dish this season," he remains hopelessly romantic by imagining
"they had walked ... a strip of the street together."[15] As he
walks, alone, the day gathers clouds until finally day struggles
with night, and light and dark themselves seem shadowy and
unreal. As he stands in front of the New Theater on the *Augus-
tusplatz*, watching until the last person enters the building, his
depression after that becomes a rare and realistic assessment of
his own prospects: "as he strode through the darkness, he admitted that, all day long, he had been cheating himself in the
usual way.... It was the old story: he played at expecting a
ready capitulation of the whole—gods and men—and, at the
same time, was only too well aware of the laborious process
that was his sole means of entry and fellowship."[16] This turns

into a letter home and finally into a dream that forces him awake in the morning.

The dream sequence, later used extensively in the trilogy, becomes an endless symbolic search for recognition on the streets of a foreign town. The final confrontation with a devil-like creature that rests in the middle of a street, hidden by people, is certainly the elusive art Maurice Guest seeks. But *it* seeks *him*, and the dream tells him to run from it—a carefully constructed symbol of the entanglements between passion, love, and art that Maurice Guest will be unable to separate effectively.

Like Niels, in Jacobsen's book, and like Richard Mahony, the major character of Richardson's first novel is faced with the life of his passionate mind and its romantic refusal to confront reality. And Guest's past life, as developed in the exposition, argues for this interpretation. In "Music Study in Leipzig," Richardson explains the pitfalls of music study in a foreign city, addressed to a young lady about to undertake it.[17] This, in an important sense, can be read as a picture of what will happen to a young English provincial, like Guest, who is temperamentally unsuited for competitive music study.

As the book begins to gather together the details of exposition, we discover that Maurice is a product of a father who insists "on the commonplace colour of his surroundings,"[18] and a mother whose reaction to his choice of profession was a "face [which] reflected the anger that burnt in her heart, too deep for speech."[19] His determination was fed by a local music teacher, who unhappily dismissed instruction of fundamentals for "the titillating melancholy of Slavonic dance-music"[20]—an error that was to put him at a disadvantage in Leipzig. His early acquaintance with the archetypal failure—an old man whose position was below that of a dancing master but who talked of his glorious days as a young man studying in Germany—left Maurice only more determined to cast aside compromise for the "tossings and agitations of the future."[21]

His first acquaintances at the conservatory lead him toward a future of dedication and a realization of where he must begin: to learn, all over again, what it meant to be a good pianist. This must be completed under Schwartz, the only master in Leipzig whose instruction would demand technique and yet retain the *"temperament* of the student." While this is reinforced by Dove, a fellow countryman of the same age, it is made blatantly clear by Schwartz in the first interview: "For you know nothing, or, let us say, worse than nothing, since what you do know, you must make it your first concern to forget...."[22]

Immediately after this, Louise enters for her daily lesson with Schwartz. All that has happened to Maurice up to this point spells an affirmative beginning. As Elizabeth Odeen indicates, he has met the instructor who will demand the most of him.[23] But just after Schwartz reminds Maurice of the tasks ahead, Maurice's passion for Louise Dufrayer begins. The focus is immediately on her eyes; and the eyes become a metaphor of beauty and impenetrable darkness that pervade his love. It is also a continuing preoccupation in Henry Handel Richardson's "shield of privacy" in her personal life and in her projection of Mahony's fears of the eyes that "spy" and "probe" in *Ultima Thule*. But at this point, Maurice only sees passionate beauty:

And then her eyes! So profound was their darkness that when they threw off their covering of heavy lid, it seemed to his excited fancy as if they must scorch what they rested on; they looked out from the depths of their setting like those of a wild beast crouched within a cavern; they lit up about them like stars, and when they fell, they went out like stars, and her face took on the pallor of early dawn.[24]

Immediately after this, Maurice experiences the first evening performance by Schilsky, and the dramatic irony is complete. Schilsky, as the artist of genius, will confront Maurice's love for Louise from the beginning to the end of the novel, and with this, will be Louise's, as Cosima's, Nietzschean dedication to the talented of the world over the mediocre. And the clues are not lost on Maurice from the beginning; Louise enters the concert hall as Schilsky is playing "with the raptness of a painted saint: her whole face listened, the tightened lips, the open nostrils, the wide, vigilant eyes." The juxtaposition of "painted" and "saint" carefully foreshadows what Elizabeth Loder defines as the fatal woman.[25] Louise is "painted" and demonic; yet she is saintly in Maurice's eyes and becomes herself a saint. As

Maurice sees her, then, at the *Abendunterhaltung,* enraptured with Schilsky's talent, Richardson intends us to see that Louise was not responsible for the evil that drove Maurice to suicide, but from the beginning was a masked, weak, and suffering woman. Henry Handel Richardson says in her 1887 diary (July 20 entry): "If only I could find the *reality!* I *wonder* if it is to be found."[26] This indicates, quite early in Richardson's life, how the moods of Louise and Maurice rest with her ultimate questioning about the nature of contrary forces hidden within the self. Leonie Kramer, by personal interview and in her book on Richardson, supports this with the statement that Henry Handel Richardson was "skilled in reconstruction rather than in creation."[27] This is supported, as well, by Green's comment that from her very earliest writing, including her first prose attempts, Richardson was intent on tracing the source of her own melancholy within her major characters.

Maurice's initial encounter with Louise is contrasted in the next chapter with his deepening relationship with Madeline Wade. But even this is interrupted by a chance meeting with Schilsky and Louise. Madeline characterizes Louise for Maurice as a pupil with "some talent, but [who] is indolent to the last degree, and only works when she can't help it. Also she always has an admirer of some kind in tow."[28] Maurice returns home with Louise's name on his lips. What begins as a novel of milieu and quickly becomes dominated by the theme of the artist as failure gains its final thematic statement as a sophisticated and ingenious naturalistic study of a man's consuming love for a woman who never returns that love. Once Maurice decides to return to kiss "the gravel where he thought she had stood,"[29] we discover what Manning Clarke describes as the "complex fate" in Richardson's art.[30] The novel becomes a dual study of failure in love and failure in art, whose protagonist refuses to compromise either.

III   *Method*

Maurice Guest is also a novel that combines the difficult task of presenting alternative dream and reality sequences through the mind of the main character. A specific technique is employed to carry out this end: first a mood, a situation, or an event is sketched indirectly and then a later, detailed explanation follows. The rationale for such a technique is to catch the reader's attention and, through the explanations that follow, to deepen the reader's understanding of the situation. For example, the romantic impulse which drives Maurice to study in Leipzig is contrasted to his vision of both an old musician in his hometown and the gray anonymity of school teaching which has swallowed up his father. Actual dream sequences also occur but not with the sophisticated interpretation familiar to readers of Joyce or Woolf. Instead, they appear curiously stiff and clumsy.

Flexibility is the key to skillful transitions between dreams and actual events. Richardson is in the process of learning her craft, and as in her use of the symbolic woods and seat in the park where Maurice and Louise first meet and where Maurice commits suicide, the method appears labored.

By contrast, Richardson's use of secondary characters appears to be immensely effective. Employing the Jamesian technique of reflectors, she uses irony to portray Dove—one reflection of Maurice's opposite—who is the student who "knew all that went on, and the affairs of everybody, as though he went through life garnering in just those little facts that others were apt to overlook." Madeline Wade, the other secondary character that reflects a way of life for Maurice, is summed up by her own characteristic statement that each day had to be "mapped and planned" in advance. To Madeline, Maurice also *reveals* as he reflects; his attractive naturalness in the early part of the book and his intense lack of sophistication are just the elements that make him attractive to her. Still another reflector character is Ephie Cayhill, who serves as a mirror to Maurice's "naturalness," lack of common sense, and lack of sophistication. Not only is she associated with a vision of existence that associates itself with the dream, but she relates to Schilsky much in the same way that Maurice relates to Louise. Schilsky lets her believe she will marry him, just as Maurice is led to believe that, once "captured," Louise will never leave him. Ephie's and Maurice's common characteristics are brought together structurally when Schilsky has a brief affair with Ephie, and Maurice's "dream love" for Louise forces him to degrade the American girl.

"Naturalness" and "innocence" destroy each other. Maurice goes to Louise's apartment with Ephie knowing she will be humiliated into an admission of an affair with Schilsky. This will shatter Ephie just as intensely as putting a bullet to her brain. And just as he has destroyed Ephie, his "naturalness" makes him tell Louise that Schilsky has returned to Leipzig. This, in a sense, "puts" a bullet in his brain as the book ends.

Louise, on the other hand, is not a reflection but an idealism in love—a pure dream. Structurally, this conception of Louise works skillfully against the harshest contrasts of dream and reality—Louise's love and sacrifice for Schilsky. Like an innocent whose personality is split between the dream of elation in love and the despair of a real jealousy, Maurice, unlike his rival, gradually renounces his professional desires for Louise. In this way, Richardson tests the validity of her theme: Schilsky, intense and realistic about his art, is annoyed when Louise interferes with his work hours. Maurice, by contrast, interrupts his work hours with the pursuit of Louise. And surrounding this contrast of single characters, the youthful tensions of the entire conservatory is developed.

Nights at the opera, evening student gatherings, departures and arrivals of couples are all communicated as large-scale reflections of the heightened tensions of students in the competitive art of music. Just as the dream and reality sequences employ a specific structural technique, these sequences begin with a straightforward account of the general tension and then a follow-up account of what caused the various attitudes underlying them. While this achieves objectivity, in its attempts to avoid authorial intrusion it seems at times more reportorial than fictional. It also points to Richardson's need for study and use of the stream of consciousness employed by Joyce, Woolf, and others on the Continent. Description followed by analysis and exploitation can be effective if it retains the fictional world.

But the structural development of Maurice's life is certainly not impaired by the author's techniques in developing the total society. Part one ends with Schilsky's departure and Maurice's realistic assessment of the circumstances. Louise is unhappily in love with Schilsky but will not take Maurice seriously. The student party given to celebrate Schilsky's departure reinforces

Maurice's confrontation with his shattered dream. But this time it is a direct confrontation, and for Maurice a decline. Schilsky leaves after a cruel, deceptive involvement with Ephie Cayhill, an abandonment of Louise, and an advancement in his music. Maurice is left with a decline in his interest in music and a more realistic but more painful assessment of Louise's love for Schilsky. Part one concerns Maurice's insistent, idiotic love for an ideal and his inability to confront the impossibility of its attainment. Richardson has achieved the "high wire" balance of dream and reality with Maurice as the center of alternating states of mind.

Structurally, part two brings Maurice step by step closer to a self-knowledge that pushes dream and reality further and further apart. His real movements are toward the destruction of his reflector characters. As if he has no knowledge of Ephie as an "innocent self," one distinct side of his central self, he submits her to Louise's harassment like a robot, almost as if to show Ephie and himself at once that the world of high art and of love must destroy, eventually, "naturalness" and "innocence." His real self knows certainly that this will bring him no closer to Louise, and yet all his dreams of her have been enchantment with an object of flowerlike beauty—his "dream self." He cannot destroy his own innocence by forcing Ephie to see that she has been fooled by Schilsky; he can only force her departure from Leipzig. Ephie lashes out at him just as Louise had done to her, and, filled with the realities of a painful emotional lesson, she leaves the city in a state of collapse. Maurice, of course, remains, now only to care for Louise. He has learned nothing.

Maurice's other major reflector, Madeline Wade, tells him that he not only acted irresponsibly but showed his "natural" self to the poorest disadvantage, and that he should have learned a lesson; for he was the type of man women took advantage of—"a mean advantage, you know. . . ." Her bluntness is intended to bring Maurice back both to his real self and the real circumstances of his career. It also shows Madeline's realistic concern for him as she attempts to interest him in setting up a music school with her in England or Australia, rather than thinking of Louise or a career as a concert pianist. She knows herself, as by this time Maurice should be able to assess himself and his capabilities. To this end, she asks Maurice's advice about the offer she has been given to stay on another year at the conservatory. His reply, however, is glossed with the self of the dream. He wants her to stay on, but for her own sake; his sole concern is for Louise's health but in only a superficially real sense. Whereas he should become Madeline's willing partner, he instead becomes Louise's caretaker in an attempt to bring her around to his concept of a relationship that will fuse "dream" and "reality." Another reflector, Dove, simply congratulates himself on escape from his innocence. When he learns that Ephie has been having an affair with Schilsky, his sense of her foolish innocence, which is Maurice's foolishness over Louise, makes him see Ephie as no partner at all.

Before part three begins, Maurice pushes his sense of the real beyond any logical turning point and creates both the character and plotting crisis of the novel. Richardson shows her major character, when faced with the realization that Louise never cared for him, about to "escape" into action on this realization. After returning from a rest in Dresden, Louise asks his advice about a proposal of marriage from a wealthy American she met there. She has resisted his attempts to fashion her life around his sense of order and simply given in because it is easier to let him care for her, put her affairs back in order, and give in to solitary walks and a chance to restore her health. But she has repeatedly made it clear that even as a friend she only accepts him grudgingly. It is peace she wants, for she is bound up in the egocentricity of the artist-lover; she makes clear to him her attitude: " 'It's myself I think of first and foremost, and as long as I live, it will always be myself." And this egocentricity is also amoral; it clings, like the artists in the novel, to whatever will make a painful moment, day, or month more livable. Louise knows she will not accept the proposal of marriage; she is waiting for Schilsky; and when Maurice, aware finally of her lack of interest in him, announces he will leave Leipzig, she launches into a second period of loneliness. The result is a series of farewells that easily seduce Maurice into the sensual enraptment that he mistakenly meshes with the self of the dream. He has always been sexually attracted to

Louise, but has never loved her. Yet Maurice fails to realize this fact. The crisis of the novel comes when, committing his fatal mistake, he goes off on a three-week idyll of sensual fulfillment in Rochlitz. He has left his career behind. Louise has someone to fill her hours before Schilsky returns, and she is content.

Structurally, the third part of *Maurice Guest* acts out the result of Maurice's mistake. Since his choice runs continually against the real self, the dream disintegrates into a sensuality that never replaces the true fidelity he expects of the relationship. But then he is mistaken again; in relinquishing his ambition as a musician for Louise's "love," he is confronted again and again with her lack of interest in working out the relationship Madeline could have given him. Only Madeline is disappointed at his poor performance at the recital; when he asks Louise how he compares with Schilsky, she says simply that Schilsky was a genius. As the fourth part continues, Maurice lashes out at her—beaten, comprehending her but still unable to understand his own motivations. Nothing is left but the utter renunciation of the sense of the real and the dream of his former self. His money is cut off; he gives up all work on his music; and when Schilsky returns, as if to torture himself, he tells Louise and she leaves him. The resolution of the action is suicide because he has failed to reorder his idealism, and he cannot reconcile the art of love, the sensual, and the work of the artist in any new perspective.

IV   *Sources*

Quite obviously, Henry Handel Richardson's period as a music student at Leipzig provided firsthand experience of the town, the operation of the conservatory, the students, and the instructors. But two other influences are important in an understanding of the sources of this novel: her future husband and the nineteenth-century European novel. Robertson not only encouraged her to write but made the initial suggestion that she write a book centered around her Leipzig experiences. He also supplied her with books by European authors, such as Flaubert and Dostoevski. Her absorption of these novelists and their novels is, essentially, what made *Maurice Guest* a European novel not in line with the current English novel at the turn of the century. In "Some Notes on My Books," she tells us that, "for the first time,... I had books in abundance: Russian, French, Danish, Norwegian, in the admirable translations for which the Germany of that time was famous. And how I read! The hour-long grind of scales and exercises passed in a flash with, say, a play of Ibsen's or a volume of Tolstoi propped open on the rack."[31]

Her interest in Flaubert came, first, from a reading of his life and letters. From this she learned how to present a story without sentimental or moral elements; and from Zola she learned how the novel must be a scientific examination of the subject.[32] Certainly her use of passionate love—its causes and its final effects—does follow French writers in contrast to the English novelists, who were unaware of the specific treatment of such a subject: "Morbid, depressing, dull, verbose, degraded, coarse, erotic, and neurotic were some of the adjectives applied to this book, built on European lines, with which, in my ignorance, I had invaded pre-war England."[33]

Secondly, her use of the femme fatale, an influence of the Decadent Movement, is certainly revealed in the fortunes of Louise Dufrayer, who, as Elizabeth Loder points out, can be compared to Swinburne's Faustine or Dolores or to the "transmutation of the Byronic Hero into Rochester or Jane Eyre."[34] But the Russian influence is evident as well, through Dostoevski: Maurice lacks strong aims and convictions and has the same fascination with love that Raskolnikov has with murder. Both men suffer from a fear—Raskolnikov, that his crime will be discovered, Maurice, that Louise will learn Schilsky has returned—that forces them to bring about their ultimate loss.

A second similarity with *Crime and Punishment* is Richardson's use of dreams to represent Maurice's psychological states of mind. Maurice's "lilac dream" is a fine example since it represents Richardson's interest in psychology and in Freud's *Interpretation of Dreams*. The dream draws on the events of the previous evening, when Maurice, after waiting in vain for Louise at Madeline's flirts with Ephie while she gives him sprigs of lilac. In the dream, Ephie is transformed into Louise, and then unhappily into Madeline. As a result, the dream sums up his relationship with each of the three women in his life: a mere friendship with Ephie, a desperate infatuation with Louise, and an unwise rejection of Madeline's love. The dream is clearly a wish fulfillment dream and illustrates a realist's use of Freudian theory.

Still another influence that shows her fidelity to fact comes from Jacobsen's *Niels Lyhne*. As noted in chapter 2, Niels and Maurice have a number of characteristics in common. Aside from simply coming to terms with life, both dream of artistic success, both are certain that with time they will achieve success, and for both, time is not enough. Both, as well, are defined in terms of their relationships with women. The resemblances between *Maurice Guest* and *Frau Marie Grubbe* remain minor.

Perhaps an even more prominent influence is the German romantic tradition, in which two movements can be distinguished: the problems of "problematical natures" and those of the artist in a society rooted in Goethe and the *Sturm and Drang* movement. For German writers of the romantic school the movement focused on the pursuer of unattainable ideals, who was usually an artist asserting the demands of his own genius against the demands of society. Goethe's *Tasso*, the first attempt to treat the problem of the artist in a contemporary manner, shows that the conflict between the artist and society seemed inevitable. The romantic school carried the issue even further: the artist was seen as the only true human being and was allowed to live in continual contact with a higher world, with his imagination as the base. Goethe's *Heinrich von Ofterdingen*, in contrast to his *Wilhelm Meister*, illustrates the inner spirit of this world in the extreme.

Henry Handel Richardson did not depend exclusively on such earlier romantic interpretation but did believe that the artist's duty to art came before his duty to society. Schilsky, of course, is the typical romantic artist while Krafft shows the influence of another German writer, Nietzsche. A. D. Hope claims that the novel's source is basically a dramatization of Nietzsche's contrast between "free" and "servile" spirits.[35]

Whatever sources influenced *Maurice Guest*, certainly Henry Handel Richardson's debt to the European novelists and writers

—particularly Flaubert, Zola, Jacobsen, Goethe, and Nietzsche— is strong but not overburdening. The novel stands, as well, as an autobiographical novel. But finally it must be considered a brilliant first novel, carefully fusing the experiences as described in *Myself When Young* with the imaginative genius of a unique talent.

CHAPTER 4

The Getting of Wisdom

I Summary and Introductory Analysis

*T*he *Getting of Wisdom* (1910), Henry Handel Richardson's second novel, describes the coming of age of a young girl in a Melbourne boarding school. Laura Rambotham, the heroine, is quickly involved in the traditions and the escapades of a "ladies college" of the late nineteenth century. Laura is first introduced telling stories to her sister and other young friends before she leaves for school. Her ability for storytelling is immediately apparent. In the same way, the book ends with hints from her schoolmates that she will write books about her travels "for us stay-at-homes," even though she denies it.[1] Richardson intended the novel to be in part "the portrait of the artist as a young child." The book ends with Laura's run down Central Avenue, away from her sister and the school, around a "sudden bend in the long, straight path," until she is lost from sight. Wisdom-getting has been a burden to be released from.

While *The Getting of Wisdom* intends to satirize the nineteenth-century school idea of memorizing facts as a way of learning, it involves distinct "tests" to be passed.[2] Each test directs Laura closer to her understanding of the nature of self and society. Initial anxieties and shyness, together with early friendships, are preludes to the lesson of the first test: "the unpardonable sin is to vary from the common mould." She prefers Thalberg to the sonatas and sonatinas of the school's music program, flaunts her ability to sight-read music, and openly asks questions about the statue of Dante and the books in the principal's study. As a result, she is soundly criticized for "the boldness of her behaviour" and all the sheet music brought from home is taken away from her. Laura learns, in other words, that "if you had abilities that others had not, you concealed them, instead of parading them under people's noses."[3] As Dorothy Green indicates in *Ulysses Bound*, Laura's education, from this first test to the last, is the result of both "enlightenment"—which is rapid, cumulative understanding—and "slow, painful experience"—which must be the definition of the getting of wisdom.[4] Concealing one's abilities comes as a lesson both in wisdom and enlightenment, and the final choice of title for this book reflects both processes.

Laura's next lesson surrounds the public expulsion of Annie Johns, a classmate not as well off as the others, who has stolen money from the richer girls. Since Laura can identify with Annie to the point of understanding "what it would mean to lack your train fare," she begins to question the basic issues of right and wrong. It is clear "the money had been taken, without exception, from pockets in which there was plenty." It is also clear that Laura feels no lasting pity for Annie, but gains a new knowledge about society. As Green says, Laura does not judge and certainly never considers acting upon what she knows to be wrong: "However miserable Laura is, she observes herself being miserable, stores up responses for later use and is unable to come face to face with a situation without the artist's mediating eye."[5] Laura's second lesson, then, gains in complexity as her school years progress. She is led to ask "that she might be preserved from having thoughts that were different from other peoples'; that she might be made to feel as she ought to feel, in a proper, ladylike way." But she also discovers how people are placed in society by others. She is criticized by her friend Tilly for staring at Annie Johns the moment she is dismissed by Mr. Strachey, and Laura relates it to a performance of Hamlet seen as a child at a Ballarat theater. To sum up, "...she watched, lynx-eyed, every inch of Annie John's progress."

Soon after the questions of right and wrong are left open to her, Laura finds herself viewed as a kind of thief. She is invited to spend the weekend at the home of Mr. Shepard, a curate, who has been the object of her own infatuations. To Laura's surprise, she discovers the man to be bad-tempered and generally unattractive. His behavior destroys any childlike fantasies, but

Laura invents a story for her schoolmates that Shepard has a
secret passion for her because of an unhappy home life. When
her lie is exposed, she is ostracized. Laura returns, in a circle
of irony, back to the lonely and despised position she found herself in when she first arrived at school. Her third phase of coming of age has taken place. She discovers how easy it is for her
quick, imaginative mind to invent new "realities." Indeed, reality,
she discovers, rests upon convincing elaboration and fusion of
truths, facts, and the imagination. After being ostracized, Laura
spends the holidays at a watering place on the bay, where one
of her aunts has a cottage. Again she confronts the idea that "if
you imagine a thing with sufficient force, you can induce your
imagining to become reality," but "the difficulty was to know
when to stop." The sea becomes a healing force, but it also
rounds off this phase in her gaining of life's wisdom.

So far as she has been obsessed with a feeling for the need to
belong. This has often become a need for a symbolic "home"
within the school society—certainly a part of the initiation process. But struggling against this are innermost feelings and
sympathies that lie outside those of the majority. At this stage
in her school career, then, Laura realizes that she will never
be able to change her innermost thoughts but must allow them
to live side by side with actions, words, and poses that represent
herself within the conventions of society. And yet, as Green
indicates, there is a final shape to this stage: she can turn "to a
milieu which she can shape as she wants it, the world of fantasy."
And the sea, as she looks out over it, "is the reconciling symbol
of the 'nomad' and the 'settler.' "[6]

. . . she fell into the habit of making up might-have-beens, of
narrating to herself how things would have fallen out, had her
fictions been fact, her ascetic hero the impetuous lover she made of
him.—In other words, lying prostrate on the sand, Laura went on
with her story.[7]

When Laura returns to school, her friends persuade her of the
"social usefulness of telling the truth." Her past lying, which is
often referred to as a "crime" just as Annie Johns's thievery,
Laura discovers to be "criminal" to the preservation of order
in society:

In these days she was for ever considering what she ought to do, what to leave undone. She learnt to weigh her words before uttering them, instead of blurting out her thoughts in the childish fashion that had exposed her to ridicule; she learnt, too, at least, to keep her real opinions to herself, and to make those she expressed tally with her hearers'.[8]

But she is now unsure how storytelling relates to the art of making literature. She is now "a regular tactician" of life and of its truths, but she still does not know how "the truth of real life [is] related to the truth of literature."[9] Her "regeneration" into society rests on understanding this clearly. She is invited to join the Literary Society by Cupid and Mary, her friends, because "she could make verses, and was also very fond of reading." She reads omnivorously, often even while pretending to practice her scales on the piano, and her reading frequently clouds the primary question of "truth" and "lying" in literature. Each book she picks up, and in the order in which she reads them, is almost a cross-section of literary initiation. *Faust* she puts down "with a kind of dreary wonder why such a dull thing should be great." Richardson's use of it in shaping *The Getting of Wisdom* is ironic in light of Laura's comment, since *Faust* poses the very complexities of permanence and transience that form a part of Laura's initiation. *Faust,* one of the works that occupied J. G. Robertson's life, certainly influenced Henry Handel Richardson's decision to place it here, and to show that while Laura was not ready to see herself as eternal "nomad" and "settler," Henry Handel Richardson was interested that we see her in that light.[10]

Ibsen's *A Doll's House* is the second book she reads as a part of her literary initiation. Aside from the obvious parallels between the names and the two heroines, Laura calls the play a "rendering of pretty things. All these people seemed eternally to be meaning something different from what they said; something that was forever eluding her." She seeks, instead, for the third book, Longfellow's romantic *Hyperion,* and goes the way of what must become further initiation: "she sought not truth, but the miracle."

Her entrance into the Literary Society depends upon a literary composition, and each of her phases of reading nicely parallels this important test. Her first is "a romance of Venice, with abundant murder and mystery in it." This is a failure, and she is advised to write about what she knows. Laura's second effort, then, is a realist's raw materials: "A Day at School." This is an overfaithful "transcript of actuality." This, too, is a failure and Cupid, who has just told her to write about what she knows, now says, "You don't need to be all true on paper, silly child!" Aside from the fact that Cupid is a nicely ironic choice of name for Laura's mentor of the romantic and the real, Laura's third composition combines "telling the truth in real life, and telling the truth in fiction." "Not a word of her narration was true, but every word of it might have been true."[11] The story combines an accurate description of the hills that surrounded Warrenega with make-believe adventure, drawn from "the caves and rocky hills where blackfellows were said to have hidden themselves, in early times." Cupid's response to this is: ". . . you know now, what it is to be true, not dull and prosy."

What does Laura conclude?

In your speech, your talk with others, you must be exact to the point of pedantry, and never romance or draw the long-bow or else you would be branded as an abominable liar. Whereas, as soon as you put pen to paper, provided you keep one foot planted on probability, you might lie as hard as you liked: indeed, the more vigorously you lied, the louder would be your hearers' applause.[12]

Her initiation into the real and fantastic has been complete, but it has all been graspings, shiftings, and sortings out of the *brain*. Her final test and initiation must be a lesson of the *feelings*. While feelings and thoughts are juxtaposed throughout the novel to reveal a whole person being shaped, Laura's passionate attachment to an older girl, Evelyn Souttar, sums up her capacity both for affection and jealous possessiveness. Earlier in the book, she has been disappointed over her love for her classmate Tilly's cousin Bob. The result of that was her imaginary infatuation with the curate. And finally that failure takes her to Evelyn Souttar, which in turn lays the groundwork for her last, most important piece of wisdom: nothing in life is permanent. As an imaginative, artistic girl, she is tragically disappointed but dangerously close to the wisdom of Maurice Guest and Richard Mahony. Since man has no real capacity to control events, they reason, the world becomes a place, in Leonie Kramer's words, of "inevitable disillusionment, dissatisfaction, and loss."[13] And as Green contends, "this is the principal piece of 'wisdom' which Laura acquires at school: the recognition of the eternal flux, *panta rei*. She also acquires some dim apprehension of its necessary rightness."[14] But this last bit of wisdom—which becomes a brief infatuation with God—rests only with the impending failure of her final term examinations. But the separation from Evelyn rests deeply with what has obviously become a lesbian relationship in Laura's clouded mind. Change, then, is positive, just as her cheating on the history examination becomes ultimately positive. But that good may come out of evil is a shock to her sense of God's workings:

A further effect of the approaching separation was to bring home to her a sense of the fleetingness of things; she began to grasp that, everywhere and always, even while you revelled in them, things were perpetually rushing to a close; and the fact of them being things you loved, or enjoyed, did not, in the least, diminish the speed at which they escaped you.[15]

It is interesting that, as Laura's infatuation with faith grew, "it was to Christ she turned by preference, rather than to the remoter God the Father."[16] Her reason is that God the Father is threatening to her both as a fatherless child and as a young girl desperately in need of the attentions of young males. God the Father she pictures "with a disagreeable, haughty look in his eyes. Christ, on the other hand, was a young man, kindly of face, and full of tender invitations." She has never had a father, and she certainly does not want a harsh one; and praying to him for passing her examinations is in a real sense praying for the study time lost while she was infatuated with Evelyn. Christ, combined with a great deal of study, saw her through all examinations properly except history. With history, He allowed her to cheat by seeing a question and then taking a book into the examination room that would answer it. She was indignant that Christ would let her do that, and she concluded that he gave her the option so she could remain a sinner. Once the shock is over, she settles down "to practise religion after the glib and shallow mode of her friends."[17]

Laura gains wisdom, then, about the nature of permanence, art and reality, and society. Truth is bound up in the art of living. As she concludes to her friends, "Oh, and that's probably what it means, too, when you say: Honesty is the best Policy."[18] Art and reality also become a sophisticated comment on the craft of realistic fiction. As Henry Handel Richardson says in "Some Notes on My Books," "Did one set out to tell a tale, though nothing in it *need* be true, everything must sound as if it were."[19] It is, then, to a *certain extent*, a portrait of the artist as a young girl. And finally, her wisdom of the eternal flux of life becomes central to all other experience.[20]

As Laura ends her school days by running down Central Avenue and disappearing out of sight, with Pin left holding her sister's hat, gloves, and leather bag, we see her rushing from the confining permanence of one existence into the certain change she now knows to be a fact of life. She is "the outsider" at her earliest stage of existence who has struggled with the nature of truth, fact, imagination, and love and found them slippery, and ultimately, overwhelming.

CHAPTER 5

The Fortunes of Richard Mahony

I Australia Felix: *Summary and General Critical Analysis*

STRUCTURALLY, *Australia Felix*, published in 1917 as Richardson's third novel, is centered around the growth of Ballarat and Richard Mahony's movement from storekeeper on the diggings to influential doctor at the center of the town's activities. Taken as a social history of the Ballarat gold diggings of the 1850s, the novel forms a panoramic structure, with an extensive range of characters and social levels. The principle of unity is inclusive rather than exclusive, even though Richard Mahony emerges as the central character nearly to the exclusion of all the others by the third volume of the trilogy. The structure could also be considered to follow Forster's "grand chain" structure,[1] since Mahony is introduced to a vast country and society, experiences a series of adventures, and ends the volume with a return trip to the part of the world he disliked a few years earlier.

Richardson's use of crowded *dramatis personae* is evident from the opening of the novel. She begins by describing the diggings themselves, with a general picture of the variety of men working at the diggings. There is Long Jim, the London lamplighter who has just lost his digging partner in a landslide. His partner, Young Bill, is characterized as a young man with "fine-gentleman airs" and "lily-white hands and finical speech," who is beaten by the hard conditions. Purdy Smith parallels Long Jim in social background—lower-class Dublin—just as Richard Mahony appears to parallel Young Bill.

The people who inhabit Ballarat, Geelong, and Melbourne are all representative of the diverse origins of those who landed in Australia in the 1850s. There is Ocock, the shrewd, crooked lawyer who sees a vast practice and vast sums of money from mining stock; Turnham, the political opportunist; Purdy Smith, the lower-class romantic who believes in the dreams of the gold diggings; Polly (Mary) Turnham, Mahony's wife, and the Beamish girls, who have come to Australia as young lower-class girls seeking wealthy husbands; Bolliver, the common Britisher who is unable to win even a meager living from the businesses of trade in Australia; Tangye and Mahony, who both reject Australia; and Sara Turnham, the old maid who teaches school but who is constantly coming and going in her search for a husband in the new Australian environment.

Just as Richardson uses the technique of crowded *dramatis personae*, she also presents her panoramic structure as it reflects the life of Richard Mahony and the characters of all social levels and backgrounds. Part one describes the people of the panorama of Melbourne and, by extension, Geelong; it follows Mahony's career from his position as bachelor storekeeper to his marriage. Each part culminates in some major change in the life of Mahony and the society at large. Part two, for example, follows the growth of Ballarat as a community with descriptions of the Eureka Stockade and a trial in Melbourne, which provides a sampling of clever lawyers and the nature of colonial justice. At the same time, it exhibits the striking contrast between Polly's and Richard's personalities, which becomes a division in the book and provides for much of the action which brings about the downfall of Mahony at the end of the third volume. The conclusion of part two is Mahony's decision to start a practice in Ballarat instead of returning to England. This decision has in reality been urged upon him by Polly, who plays a greater and greater influence upon his decisions as the book progresses. Throughout part two, the extensiveness of the structure is indicated by pictures of childbirth and death in Australia of the 1850s—Polly's unfortunate struggle in childbirth and Emma Turnham's death.

Part three extends the panoramic structure by illustrating the specifics of Ballarat's growth as a mining community; Mahony reflects the happenings of the society in general with the slow but steady growth of his practice and by his investments in mining stock which, at the end of part three, yield him two thousand pounds. And Mahony is concerned with all the pressing intellectual issues of the day. As such, he is part of Richardson's attempts to create a panoramic structure of the life and thought of the times. And there are other indications through descriptions of the emerging and descending social classes. Glendinning, a pioneer squatter, is described as dying of alcohol, the result of years of isolation in the Australian bush. Henry Ocock, the opportunistic lawyer, is revealed as a part of the activities of the emerging social classes over the dying efforts of the original squatters. The panorama of Ballarat West is recorded in all its aspects: the elections for Parliament, a typical convenience marriage of the colonies between Tilly Beamish and old Mr. Ocock, the convalescence marriage between John Turnham and Jinny Beamish, and a general picture of colonial hospitality.

Part four, the last part of the book, describes the coming of age of Ballarat as a city and ends in Mahony's return to England. It describes the prosperity and social and material escalation of the newly rich colonials in the Victoria province of the 1850s and 1860s. The Mahonys' house, for example, is on Webster Street, and twice as big as their old one; "People had gone up, gone down—had changed places like children at a game of General Post"; and Henry Ocock's holdings make him the wealthiest man in Ballarat. Old Devine, Polly's onetime market gardener, has made thousands and is being considered for Parliament. Mahony's practice takes giant strides. But Ned, Mahony's brother-in-law, takes a turn downward and is forced to marry the daughter of a public housekeeper from the mining population of Castlemaine. And almost as a conclusion to part four, the Mahonys hold an elaborate "musical" party. The party includes the moneyed of Ballarat but social backgrounds ranging from the Devines to John Turnham. Those who have reached the depths of a "downward direction" are also included. Mahony, for example, talks with Tangye and learns about the frustrations of this poor proprietor of a chemist's shop who has found only failure and depression in Australia. Mahony's interest in securing an assistant for his growing practice brings him upon another specimen—a man named Wakefield who has been crushed by a poor reputation. But other Ballaratians are "attending the Melbourne race metings; the Government House balls and lawn parties; bringing back the gossip of Melbourne, together with its fashions in dress, music, and social life."[2]

Part four culminates in a ball which had "been organized to raise funds for a public monument to the two explorers, Burke and Wills; and was to be one of the grandest ever given in Ballarat."[3] The aftermath of the ball adds still further to the extensiveness of the book's structure. It indicates how much the Ballarat ball was a high point in all the characters' lives. Purdy, the typical caricature of the footloose, mindless personality that comes to dig gold, makes improper advances to Mary at the Ball. This action causes the first clear split between Mary and Richard and discloses the basic differences in their personalities. Mahony has a severe case of sunstroke while returning from a patient; this results in a long convalescence, including a month on the seacoast. Deaths are recorded: Mr. Ocock's and Jinny's. Friendships are broken: Henry Ocock turns away from Mahony because the doctor tells him his wife drinks too much, and Purdy leaves Ballarat, robbing Mahony of the one friend he knew from childhood remaining in Australia. Both Ocock's severing of ties and the loss of Purdy's friendship causes Mahony infinite restlessness and finally drives him back to England.

II   Australia Felix: *Patterns of Character and Structure*

Instead of *telling* us about the contrariness of Mahony's nature, Henry Handel Richardson shows us, through countless scenes in which Mahony is described in all the curious aspects of his nature. In the first volume, he emerges rather slowly as the man who has significant concerns that are not shared by the other people at Ballarat. He asks himself early in the first volume: "What am I? Whence have I come? Whither am I going? What meaning has the pain I suffer, the evil that I do?"[4]

Mahony goes through various kinds of frustrations in the first volume as he addresses himself to his questions. When he has decided to go along with Polly and John and start a medical practice in Ballarat, he asks himself whether or not a Power works outside himself. When he returns to a study of biblical criticism and scientific inquiry, he confronts himself with these same basic questions and is reassured by a kinship with the Eternal and with all created things. When he gains two thousand pounds in mining stock at the same time as his medical practice increases, he marvels at the building of success upon explainable success. And when he reaches middle age and decides to return to England, God no longer has an answer as he asks the most basic of questions: why is life left empty, and why must this recognition be painfully sudden?

All levels of the *Australia Felix* world have their types, and each of the minor characters serve as reflectors to Mahony's vision of Australia: the diggers who never give up the dream of easily won gold—Ned, Johnny, and Purdy; the digger who gives up the dream—Long Jim; the emerging professionals, with their various shades of opportunism—Henry Ocock, John Turnham, and even Archbishop Long; the frustrated failures of colonization—Glendinning, Tangye, Bolliver, Wakefield, and Brace; the wives, the results of the flexible conditions of a rapidly emerging society—Agnes, Mrs. Urquart, Jinny, Tilly, and Amelia, to name a few; and the old maid in search of a husband—Sara; and many more. It is enough to say that all of Richardson's secondary characters can be described in one sentence—they all contrast or reinforce sides of Mahony's character.

In handling the action, Henry Handel Richardson adds plot-interest to story-interest. Early in the first part, the reader asks himself whether Mahony will stay in Australia or leave and whether Mary will prevent Richard from making the actual move as the book ends, based on what we know of Mary's growing capabilities in dealing with Richard. We find that she has grown to understand Richard as a child who needs compassion. But even more important is the question of whether or not Mahony will be satisfied anywhere, based on what has already been presented of his personality. The reader begins to wonder if it has not something to do with his search for the basic questions of existence.

III   Australia Felix: *The Pattern of Action*

With these basic questions in mind, let us consider how the book's tempo, flashbacks, foreshadowings, conflicts, and aura of inevitability affect the total action. The tempo, first, is clearly rapid, with broad time gaps in the course of hundreds of events that happen to the Ballarat society. The tempo indicates just

how selective Henry Handel Richardson is during the course
of Mahony's four major decisions of the book—to get married, to
go into medical practice, to move up in society as a result of a
growing practice and gains in mining stocks, and to leave for
England. The tempo up to the time of his marriage covers,
through summation of events and flashbacks, his dislike of medical practice in England, his journey to Australia, his few months
digging for gold, and his decision to set up a store on the diggings. It also covers his loss of goods due to a crooked agent,
his journey to Melbourne to secure a lawyer, his numerous
journeys to Geelong, his journey to John Turnham to secure
permission for the marriage, the marriage itself, and the long
journey back to the diggings. All these events take one hundred
and one pages; the other parts progress at approximately the
same pace.

Richardson's flashbacks rarely occur in large blocks, only in
short glimpses or through the author's commentary on what
Mahony should be remembering. Examples include Mahony's
memories of his experiences with Purdy. The use of foreshadowing, just as the use of flashback, is most pronounced in the
character of Mahony. It is clear that the growing differences
between husband and wife will lead to a quarrel, and that this
quarrel will in some way affect Mahony's decision to leave Australia. The foreshadowing for the entire character of Mahony
is also clear; in the proem to the volume, the character of Young
Bill and his confinement in the landslide is indicative of what
will happen to Mahony as the trilogy progresses.

While the major issue in the first volume is the confinement
of Australia as opposed to the freedom of England, smaller bases
of conflict come in with the conflict between Mahony and the
lower-class characters, culminating in his rejection of Purdy.
There is the gradually building conflict with his wife's opposing
personality; the conflict between Mahony's "way," and the ambitious methods of the opportunists, Henry Ocock and John
Turnham, ending in the break with the former; and the conflict between Mahony's struggles to comprehend the meaning of
God, which lead him to disagree with the biblical criticism and
evolutionary theories which he reads. All these conflicts are

inevitable in that they are produced not by coincidence but by responses to the challenge of circumstance and environment.

IV   Australia Felix: *Setting and the Effects of Richardson's Use of History on Style*

While setting functions as basic atmosphere, it is primarily viewed as an environmental force which makes men poor or rich, and which brings out their opportunism or their sensitivities. As Henry Handel Richardson tells us in "Some Notes on My Books," she is concerned with the majority of the diggers in the gold fields, and the majority failed both financially and in spiritual and physical adjustment to Australia.[5] At a time when eight tons of gold were being shipped weekly from Victoria ports, the average miner's earnings amounted to only three or four pounds a week, and these gradually decreased as the metal had to be sought at deeper levels.[6] Richardson's concern is to create a vast historical setting which shows Mahony as a man unable to adjust physically and spiritually to Australia.

Mahony is first seen in colonial Australia of the 1850s, in the midst of the early gold diggings in Victoria, specifically the diggings at Ballarat. Ever since the rush to California, a new excitement had been created by the pursuit of gold, and Australia had been the next strike. In countries the world over, industry had become consolidated, small crafts destroyed, and there were few opportunities for the man with initiative but no money. The era became one in which great numbers of men suffered from a sense of political and social frustration: in England, the Chartist movement had lingered and died, and on the Continent the abortive revolutions of the 1840s made this feeling possible. Hopes for new rewards and changes lay with the newer countries like Australia. During the 1850s, the gold from the Australian fields amounted to two-fifths of world production and was worth a hundred million pounds. The Victorian diggings alone were richer in yield than those of all California.

As a novelist, Henry Handel Richardson brings the period to life through her use of various kinds of historical detail. She introduces political history through the description of the Eureka Stockade revolt, using the firsthand account in Withers' *History* and Raffaello's *The Eureka Stockade*.[7] She describes all levels of reaction to the stockade, from Mahony's interest in law and order to Purdy's and Ned's active fighting against the military forces. Each character is representative of a specific type that came to Australia by the hundreds.

But the physical setting is just as historically representative as are the characters. She took extensive notes from every variety of source: observations of people who visited the country, colonials who wrote about settling in Australia, and even "narrative sketches" of the life of the times, together with maps of Ballarat and Melbourne at various stages of their development, photographs, and drawings of old Ballarat.[8] Using Howitt's *Two Years in Victoria* and Kelly's *Life in Victoria,* she made four large notebooks, with a full index, amounting to over three hundred pages.[9] From Howitt and Kelly, and many other sources, she assembled two kinds of material: first, the kind that can be readily seen as of great importance in the trilogy's composition, such as the description of the mines in chapter 1; and second, the kind that added to her knowledge of the times, but quite obviously could have no part in the trilogy itself, such as the information, in the second notebook, that "Oxhides are now [in the 1850s] being exported. They are salted on the spot worth from 15/18 each in the colony."[10]

What emerges is a comprehensive picture of Australia in the 1850s. From Clacy's *A Lady's Visit to the Gold Diggings of Australia in 1852–53,*[11] she learns about the actual process of digging for gold in Ballarat, and applies it to the proem to *Australia Felix.* She also made use of source material from Withers' *History of Ballarat* for views of the Australian continent in the light of English conditions and attitudes, for testimony of early settlers, squatters, and shepherds, including eyewitness accounts of the years before the gold rush. She made use of *Ballarat and Vicinity,* an account published in the late 1800s, when Ballarat was a wealthy township. Such a volume provided her with a rich vein of biographical accounts of the men who shaped the course of public affairs and with incidents sketched out that are related to the parts of the trilogy that in turn relate to the institution of law and order in the mining community. From Withers' *History,* for example, she transforms impressions of early Ballarat as it would have been viewed by early explorers into a description that accentuates the greenless, desolate, and hopeless land of the gold diggings, looking down upon "the havoc that had been made of the fair, pastoral lands."[12] From her sources in Clacy's *A Lady's Visit* . . . she attempts to describe the Ballarat gold diggings as Mahony, Purdy Smith, and old Ocock worked in them. The summer and parts of the spring leave Clacy's "fine" creeks, "small" rivers, and waterfalls in drought, with good water scarce and the water that does remain putrid and clogged with the yellow mud that clings, like gangrene, to the men and tents.[13] And when the autumn rain comes, it comes with just the intensity that Richardson describes it. The rain quickly assumes the proportions of a flood, destroying supplies, tents, and infesting the pits until working conditions are intolerable.

From this range of accumulated detail of the life of Australia in the 1850s, Richardson uses the techniques of the historical novelist to illuminate the primary mood of the times. She portrays realistically the mood of failure, futility, and confinement which led to the Eureka Stockade. And the same concentration of futility of the diggers' environment is seen in her account of the road from Ballarat to Melbourne. As Mahony and Purdy make their way to Melbourne, the author's descriptions, taken in part from her visit to Australia in 1912, but mostly from Withers's *History,* are carefully selected to show the inescapable confinement of the hell-like environment to which these men have committed their lives.

Richardson's style emerges from her attempts to set a mood, or a tone, in the setting. She writes of the changes in the whole continent as well as specific scenes incorporating dialogue and description. Generalized narrative includes the author's description of the Mahonys moving into their new home. Probably the best example of a description of an event in *Australia Felix* is the account of the Eureka Stockade incident. Still another indication of the flexibility of Richardson's style is her use of the analysis of events. Mahony's thoughts on biblical criticism and evolution, for example, reveal her effectiveness in making use of thought patterns. The opening novel of the trilogy offers numerous effective mixtures of dialogue and action that reveal an ability to portray things dramatically as well as pictorially.

V   Australia Felix: *Autobiographical Materials and the
Novel's Theme*

In this imaginative transformation of her mother and father,
Richardson has done far more than record the ups and downs of
emigrant lives; she has portrayed two of the most basic and most
universal characteristics of mankind. She contrasts her father's
search for answers to the basic questions of existence with his
wife's lack of interest in these questions. She alters the picture
of her father to reinforce the theme of failure, which represents
both a subconscious desire to make his character an image of her
literary self and the application of Zola's methods to her own
scientific realism. Nothing is more illustrative of this fact than
the recurrent images of confinement and escape.

Henry Handel Richardson hints immediately at the theme
of confinement and escape, with the initial burial alive of the
young miner, Bill, in the proem to *Australia Felix*. A friend of
Long Jim's who has much of the sensitivity and fastidiousness
of Richard Mahony, Bill is the victim of a poorly constructed
shaft which collapses under the increased weight of rain-sodden
earth. He is one of the many victims of the goldfields, just as
Mahony is one of the many victims of a medical practice which
involves impossible distances and the danger of sunstroke
through long hours under the Australian sun. Both the gold
digger who begins the story with his death, and the Australian
doctor who ends it with his escape to England, experience the
horror of confinement. While Long Jim escapes the confinement
of Australia by a trip to England, he returns; and Purdy feels a
confinement that even he is unaware of. He spends most of his
young adult years, like Ned, searching for a rich goldfield to
escape the confinement of obscurity and meager living. In this
way Richardson has intricately woven the dreams and ambitions
of the gold diggers with Mahony's, and Mahony's with all the
others who have settled in Australia.

This is the confinement of Australia that Mahony faces in the
land, the malevolent mother-goddess Australia from whom there
is no escape—all the undesirable characteristics of "the strange,
motley crowd" as well as his family, which, by his wife's continual stress on the practical and financial, thwart his chances for

escape. Mahony, like the others, had come in pursuit of the self-destructive dream, "the fantastic notion of redeeming the fortunes of his family."[14] While the idea is quickly substituted for storekeeping, the dream still remains, and he is bound for a journey of spiritual adventuring, of intellectual excitement which drives him to give up his promising medical practice in Ballarat to return to England. His wife's objections to such a move are the first signs of confinement.

VI   The Way Home: *Summary and General Critical Analysis*

The Way Home, published in 1925, has a similar panoramic structural pattern. The novel begins with Richard Mahony's arrival in England and ends with his return to Australia—a final return after twice leaving, gaining a fortune and losing it, and undertaking a grand tour of the Continent. Instead of simply changing his status in one country, Mahony makes moves from England back to Australia and then back to England again.

Part one of *The Way Home* reveals his attempts to find a medical practice in English town society and ends with his return to Australia, only to find he is a wealthy man. Part two describes the Mahonys' efforts to settle into the wealthy Melbourne society as peers, and ends in the birth of their children; Part three pictures their adjustment to the process of raising children, their other activities as wealthy Australians, and the grand tour of England and the Continent. This ends in Italy, with the telegram that sends them back to Australia nearly penniless. All these events reveal the life of the Mahony family behind a "grand chain" of events and societies, including societies never described in *Australia Felix*. The English lower class of Leicester, the English town society of Buddlecombe, the Melbourne society of wealthy Australians, and the "traveling societies" of the grand tour are all new structural frameworks. Henry Handel Richardson's attempt, as in *Australia Felix*, is to present an extensive structure with a unity of inclusion rather than exclusion. Once again, the attempt is to provide for crowded *dramatis personae* which define the societies in which the Mahonys move.

The first link in the grand chain is the society at Leicester. Starting a practice to replace Mr. Brocklebank, the surgeon "who was one of the original landmarks of the neighbourhood," Richard finds that Brocklebank's practice does not bring the wealthy leather and hose manufacturers of the town but only the common laborers. These people are representative of the English lower class manufacturing town which Richard eventually rejects. Leicester is simply another version of the Ballarat gold diggings; and Richard finds it even more deadly than the society of the diggers.

His next practice, in Buddlecombe, involves gaining the business of a few wealthy residents, most of whom look down upon his colonial background. But Richard also serves a slightly higher breed of the common people of this small, seacoast town: the huckster, publican, ostler, the Anglo-Indian officer, and the vicar's wife with her penny readings and sunday-school feasts. The two most important houses are the "Hall" and the "Court"; below them are the Challoners' of "Toplands" and Blakeneys' of the "Towers."

The town's reaction to the Mahony party—which includes a mixing of the wrong guests and too generous an amount of food— indicates the panorama of social levels. The snobbishness of the townspeople as opposed to Mary's inherent generosity forms a broadly based contrast between Australian concern for the immediate value of people and things and British concern for "presentableness," background, and other customs of the past.

But Melbourne society, like Buddlecombe society, has its own set of pretenses. There are the Devines, owners of a large mansion, with a group of servants. Devine, the old market gardener of *Australia Felix*, is now a member of the legislative council soon to form a new ministry. And there is Miss Timms-Kelly, Judge Kelly's daughter, who sings to Mahony's "obligato" on the flute; the ball at the Government House, where Mary's splendid appearance takes away the breath of an Englishman who wanders through "this colonial assembly much as a musical connoisseur might wander through a cattle yard"; and the musical party at the Timms-Kellys' with the group of "bachelors . . . past marrying age; greybeards, who, in listening to the strain of *Norme* or *Semiramide*, re-lived their youth." There is Mrs.

Phyare and her frequent seances, which result in Richard's quick adoption of the philosophy of spiritualism; and Mrs. Marriner, a rich, young widow with beauty, ease, and elegance of manner who continues Richard's interests in the seance, and shares intellectual interests. Such people contribute to an extensive picture of the rich society of Melbourne in the latter half of the nineteenth century.

The panoramic structure of the grand tour—the Mahonys' second trip to England—is contained in their manner of travel. On this second trip, they travel "in style, accompanied by a maid to attend to Mary, and both nurses"—the traditional mode of travel for the wealthy on a grand tour. They take a house for the winter in Kensington Gore, and they take walks with the children every day in Kensington Gardens. The grand tour to the Continent begins with a trip from Dover to Calais, and then on to Paris; it becomes a kind of mad race across Europe, with the whole of the Continent as a panoramic background. Their travel takes them to the busy streets of Paris, the cathedral town of Strasbourg, the Rhine, the Vosges, the Black Forest, the Tyrolese mountains, the breweries of Munich, and the Leaning Tower of Pisa.

VII The Way Home: *Structural Patterns and Point of View*

Ending with the society of the grand tour, the three-part pattern discloses the broad range of the skeletal framework. Richardson has attempted to portray three societies of nineteenth-century life in three hundred and twenty pages; and, in attempting such a task, she has necessarily been forced to condense a great deal of her picture. Much more material, for example, is narrated by the author than revealed through character and dialogue. We can see what Richardson means when she says, in "Some Notes on My Books," that she wrote the book too rapidly and wonders how it "ever got itself written at all."[15]

Any number of examples will illustrate how much Richardson intrudes upon the flow of the narrative to cover the many events of the novel. Mahony's attempt to start a practice in England, the life in Melbourne, and the life on the grand tour all include examples. Her description of the birth and early years of the

Mahonys' children, for example, is treated in one short chapter, with the summary statement at the end: "Such were Mahony's children." A series of statements in other parts of *The Way Home* will indicate to what extent her point of view is intrusive rather than neutral.

An even more revealing passage comes as Richardson comments upon Mary's role in raising the children: "She alone gave them that sense of warmth and security, in which very young things thrive."[16] A comment of this kind, while not an extended statement by the author on "how infants thrive," is an example of the author intruding upon the narrative. But still another example concerns Richard's observations and thoughts on his son: "...Mahony saw what he long remembered: a fight for self-control extraordinary in one so young."[17] Again the author is commenting upon and interpreting the event in a summary statement, rather than giving the thought completely to the character.

Perhaps one of the best examples of this is the thought "put into the mouth" of a character without the necessary transition: "...for the first time, she [Mary] did not excuse a wrong doer with a loving word. And this her own child!"[18] To whom is the author addressing the last sentence? By a stretch of the imagination, it could be Mahony, and yet the transition is by no means complete. Richardson's use of the "half-intrusive" author is primarily for a short, summary statement; her concern is not for a leisurely comment on the action and characters but for a statement that will quickly familiarize the reader with the necessary material to keep the story moving. Because she covers too much, she is forced to rely on this technique to make her characters believable and her situations convincing. Even the technique of characterization relies more on a summary statement of traits than a number of scenes revealing the character in action.

VIII   The Way Home: *Characterization*

The characterization of *The Way Home,* like the point of view, relies more on the summary statement than the subtle and gradual method of presentation. Richard and Mary Mahony "surprise in a convincing way," but they do so within the context of a swirling number of scenes and time shifts, which are sometimes so rapid that it is difficult to assimilate the nature of their change. The flat characters first introduced in *Australia Felix* retain their static characteristics but are not reintroduced, for the most part, even in the fullness of their original characterization. But there is Emmy, John Turnham's daughter by his first marriage, who had blossomed into a "simple-hearted, unaffected girl, as natural as she was pretty"; and Zara, Mary Mahony's sister, whose "dimples had run to lines, the cheeks hollowed, the skin sagged." Zara's marriage to Hempel, Richard's old assistant storekeeper on the Ballarat diggings, portrays Zara as the old maid well into middle age, who hangs on to life by marrying a man dying of phthisis. Tilly Ocock, Mary's friend from the Beamish boardinghouse days, remains central to Mary's social life but retains her loud, masculine characteristics, even in her courting and marriage to Purdy Smith. Mary's description of her as she waits for the train, ready to marry Purdy, is perhaps typical of the characterization Richardson has drawn since early in *Australia Felix*. The only sign of "decency," Mary remembers, came and went with "the decent and becoming black to which, as 'old Mrs. Ocock,' she had been faithful for so long."

John Turnham's decline and death, as well as his impossible marriage to Lizzie Kelley, continue to illustrate his characteristics as the opportunistic colonial. John's manner of dying is equally as characteristic as his life of driving ambition. As Richardson tells us, "John, believing himself alone with his maker, railed and rebelled, in blind anguish, against his fate" and "... livid, drenched in sweat, John fought his way to death through tortures indescribable."[19]

The static characters of Leicester and Buddlecombe, like those of the Australian environment, maintain an inflexible set of characteristics from the time they are introduced until they disappear from the plot altogether. Mrs. Turnham, Mary's mother, is described from the beginning as a simple, kindhearted woman concerned about the fortunes of all her children. From what we can gather, Mary seems to be a picture of her mother, but with perhaps more of an open personality.

The other characterizations at Leicester—Lisby, Bealby, and other townspeople—are of the briefest kind. Lisby appears to be the boisterous young English girl who has an opinion for everything and is not afraid to express it. Bealby is almost Dickensian in both the manner of characterization and variety of character. Perhaps the best indication of flat characterization in Buddlecombe is the household of the Saxeby-Corbetts, specifically Mrs. Saxeby-Corbett. The arrival of the family is "after the fashion of crowned heads. First came the drag-loads of servants," then the house was prepared by the servants and the people of the town—the elderly women, the tradespeople, footman, grooms, attendant governesses and nursemaids. The arrival of the lady herself is indicative of her character: ". . . lastly came his lady, driving herself in a low chaise: a bony-jawed, high-nosed woman, whose skin told of careless exposure to all weathers."[20] Her arrogance to the tradesmen of the town, her independence, and her masculine forcefulness typify a representative figure of the upper-class English town society which Mahony rejects. Although she has a competence which Mahony respects—for once, as Mary notes, "his lordly manner went down" when he was called to the Saxeby-Corbetts—she is the reason for his return to Australia.

Mahony makes daily visits to Buddlecombe Hall to care for a nursery full of children with chicken pox; he also becomes "a kind of protege of its mistress: she would keep him, after his professional visit was paid, to chat about the colonies, and hear his impressions of England."[21] These talks turn into invitations to "little informal dinners," but climax with a dinner to which Mahony is invited but not Mary. The comments just before this dinner send Richard back to Australia; at this point Richardson brings a climactic ending to Mrs. Saxeby-Corbett's characterization—an ending that reveals all the values and prejudices of the English personality.

IX   The Way Home: *Mahony as Evolving Character*

Mahony changes several times in the course of the book, as the result of ups and downs in his fortunes, but ends the book an increasingly fastidious, faddy person who has only briefly al-

,lowed himself to emerge as a likable personality. He continues to ask basic questions about the nature of existence, concluding his search in *The Way Home* with the study of spiritualism as the best source for the answers to his questions. This comes after extensive study of the pure science of his day, which he finds empty of workable solutions. His studies of spiritualism are especially valuable to him, because "they taught confidently that all life emanated from God ... to God world return, and in Him continue to exist." This assurance of a God brought Mahony what he valued most: an assurance of a Hereafter.

But Mahony is still nagged by doubts, even as he witnesses the success of seances in Melbourne and London. He ends the novel a restless, unconvinced man. He comes from Australia with high hopes of settling comfortably into an English practice and turns "sociable and hearty, taking an interest in his fellow-travelers, a lead in the diversions of the voyage." Between times he reveals both the gregarious and the angry, restless sides of his personality. This is illustrated by the sociableness of his life in Melbourne society, with the intellectual company of the bishop's circle, Lizzie Turnham, and Mrs. Marriner; and the restless fastidiousness of his ruffled dignity in Buddlecombe, when Mrs. Saxeby-Corbett discusses Mary's colonial manners. The vacillations between these two extremes characterizes Mahony as a man surprising the reader in a convincing way. As a hopeful colonial returning to England, for example, he becomes the friendliest and most helpful person aboard ship.

After a few weeks in London, "they had seen and heard enough of London to last them for the rest of their lives." The arrival in Leicester seems to provide a change. Instead of becoming lost in the strangeness of the town, or viewing it as another Ballarat, Mahony jumps at the chance of taking over old Brocklebank's practice a few days after he arrives. Such a quick judgment is criticized by Mary and even Lisby; and their judgments are borne out by Richard's leaving the practice before the year is out. Mary, of course, is thinking of the contrast between Ballarat and Leicester: "To have flung up a brilliant practice, a big house and garden, a host of congenial friends ... for this: a miserably pokey house, in a small dull street, in a dull ugly town!"[22] She decides, however, to let Richard have his way, just as she allowed him to leave Australia when she was against it. She has learned, from the first experience, that "the one way to deal with Richard was to give him his head, and only by degrees deftly trickle in doubts and scruples." No longer does she view her husband as the trustworthy, competent judge of their fortunes; from the time of their first violent quarrel, after the governor's ball in Ballarat, she has learned the necessity of manipulating Richard and hoping for the best.

X The Way Home: *Mary as Evolving Character*

At this stage in her life, Mary has become convinced that she must assert her will over Richard. She has evolved from a shy sixteen-year-old bride, worshipping her husband, to a confident, capable wife, and finally to a wife who realizes her judgment is sounder than her husband's on matters of getting on in the world. However, their unexpected wealth through mining stocks has softened her determination to control their fortunes, and she is at a loss as to how she should assert her will. The weakening that the money brings gives rise to other considerations; she realizes that "to be nothing, to have neither trade nor profession, to fold one's hands and live on one's income— that was the *ne plus ultra* of colonial society, the ideal tirelessly to be striven for."[23] And she asks herself another question: "Was anybody better fitted than Richard, by birth and breeding, to live as the gentleman?"

When the matter of living in Melbourne or in Ballarat, and of buying or building is discussed, Mary again hesitates to assert her will because money is no longer a question. As to the place they would live, "she found herself up against a stone wall, in the shape of a hitherto unsuspected trait in Richard: a violent aversion to returning on his traces."[24] Because the return to medical practice is no longer necessary, Mary can do nothing but give in to Richard's choice. But the question of buying or building is solved by an arrangement with John Turnham to have Richard look over a good prospect, react favorably to it, and decide to buy it after all. Such scheming indicates Mary's continual judgment that asserting her will is essential to making sound decisions.

The last major decision of the book—the decision to take a grand tour, and by extension, to sell the house—is a climactic example of Mary's inability to assert her will when it is most important. Her feelings against taking the trip are softened by Richard's own needs: she finds him too wrapped up in spiritualism, "turned into a bundle of credulous superstition"; and she finds him aging considerably. Her feelings are for Richard: "when it came to a question of Richard's bodily health and welfare, all other considerations must go by the board."[25] The question of the house and the changing of agents seem to catch Mary off guard. Richard had already accepted an offer from a wealthy squatter to sell the house before telling Mary what he had done.

Although Mary makes Richard promise that the money from the house will be saved for the purchase of another one upon their return, the benefit of her practical sense is lost through Richard's choice of an agent. Because he had let all his friends slip away during the years of his wealth, Mahony had only Purdy to ask about a reliable agent. When Mary hears of his source, she is extremely skeptical but can only ask Richard to check the agent over carefully before making a decision.

Because of her inability to see the gravity of the situation, she allows Richard to check with Purdy on the agent's references and to interview the agent and transact the business. From Richard's reactions, she knows he was disappointed with the agent and yet went through with the transactions, telling her: "Well, well, my dear, all our troubles are now over!" Her only recourse is to have Jerry, now a bank manager, check on the conditions of their holdings while they are away. For all her practical sense and good judgment, Mary is unable to avert the loss of their fortunes. Her judgment, like Mahony's, is unable to see the consequences of dealing with a crooked agent.

It is at this point that Mary's will is shown as unequal to many of the important practical tasks of life; and when the loss of their money is known, she begins to realize, in the last volume of the trilogy, how a commonsense approach to life cannot solve all its problems. As *The Way Home* ends, she is dimly aware of this fact of life. She realizes that life is more than practical success.

XI The Way Home: *The Use of Setting*

The use of setting in *The Way Home*, unlike *Australia Felix*, is telescopic. Throughout *The Way Home*, most of the descriptions of setting follow a threefold pattern of intensity: a description of the country, then the specifics of the town and its implications as a society, and finally a description of the setting in which the Mahonys move as a family, whether it is the house in Buddlecombe, Ultima Thule in Melbourne, or the house in Kensington Gore, or even the hotel in Venice. Part two, for example, begins with a general description of Australia through the assortment of people that meet the Mahonys as they land. Each of these people, although old friends to the Mahonys, represent some aspect of the larger colonial culture. Tilly, the young girl who succeeded in winning a man and a fortune, is dressed in her widow's weeds; John Turnham, the opportunist, who arrives "with the same old air of: I am here; all is well"; Zara, "fluttering a morsel of cambric: she had feared an attack of *mal de mer*"; Agnes Ocock and Amelia Grindle, "with sundry of their children, and the old Devines;" and Purdy, the footloose man of no fortune, with "more than a hint of coming stoutness; a cheap and flashy style of dress."

From this picture of the country through its people, Richardson focuses on one character who is perhaps symbolic of all the rest: old Devine. After their arrival, the Mahonys become guests in the Devine's house. The house is probably the best example of the meaning of this new society. Through this view of the society to which the Mahonys are now a part, Richardson focuses on the house they choose. Like the house in Buddlecombe, it represents the concept of "home" in the Melbourne of this era.

The three settings of *The Way Home*, aside from implementing the principle of spheres of intensity, also represent an effective use of environmental force. England is described as confined, condensed, and relying on the traditions of social class, background, and family distinctiveness; Australia relies upon vastness, treeless barrenness, and the sun, with the inexhaustible wealth, the tradition of lavish spending, and the gaudy display of luxury; and the grand tour is described as a never-ending line of suffocating antiquities, churches, monuments, and histories.

Such a setting reflects Richard Mahony's viewpoint; it also reflects the use of setting as an environmental force that compels Richard to delight in restless and sometimes mad travel, and to be annoyed by the confinement of England's smallness, Australia's sun, and the hotels on the Continent. Such an environmental force is best represented during the grand tour. Richard's reaction to London, for example, is typical of his desire to see everything as rapidly as possible. Aside from all the spiritualist seances Richard and Mary attend in London, there are the environmental forces of the cities of the Continent that both repel Richard and urge him on to the next city, so as not to miss anything.

Just as these discomforts and fears move Richard from one city to the next, his movement also begins to evolve into a pattern. His movement becomes a search, in the various settings of the tour, for a "home." Earlier in *The Way Home*, his attempts to start a practice in Buddlecombe had been an effort to secure a home in England, as his efforts to attach himself to the Melbourne society had been an attempt to root himself in the Australian environment. Both of these environments failed him. His grand tour of the Continent, then, becomes an effort to find a "home" that suits him in both a symbolical and a real sense; he is testing out each city of Europe for its "ability" to become a home. When he finds it wanting in any respect—we must agree that he rarely gives any of the cities an honest try—he leaves it for the next. Only Venice suits him; but a telegram from Australia that announces his financial ruin forces him to leave. Even Mary's comment on Richard's tastes indicates his interest in Venice is an interest in "home." He likes Venice, she maintains, because it seems to be a restful place. But the telegram informing him of his loss turns the setting into a nightmare and causes him to board the Overland Mail for Egypt. The environmental force, as a result, turns back on itself, making Richard return to Australia once more, against his will. All the events of the grand tour create restlessness and even panic. It is inevitable that the trip should end in castastrophe.

XII   The Way Home: *Style and Interior Monologue*

The style of *The Way Home,* like its point of view, is marred
by Richardson's practice of continually summarizing events and
scenes rather than giving them the full benefits of dialogue and
action. More specifically, the style of *The Way Home* is burdened
with generalized narrative or summary. Mahony's reading program, soon after he settles in *Ultima Thule,* is a good example
of how Richardson summarizes the passing of weeks in five and a
half pages. By devoting half a chapter to this topic, she reveals
a plotting technique that forces on the reader summaries of
events. Practically every chapter in the book announces a new
event that moves the action past days or weeks; and each chapter concerns itself with one event, "filling in" the reader on the
most important aspect of this event as it relates to the total
plotting of the book.

Because she relies on this method of letting the chapter divi-
sions form the structure for the events, Richardson forces herself into a pattern that lends itself to summary. One can almost
see her laying out her chapters in outline form: chapter six will
concern Mahony's reading; chapter seven his evenings of musical
parties at the Timms-Kellys; and so on. As a result, when we
come to Mahony's reading of the great books in the science
and philosophy of his day, we have the feeling that she will
summarize Mahony's thinking—all of his thinking—in this chapter and that it will be left to us to simply pick out the key
passages before going on to the next chapter. And indeed she
does. After telling us that Mahony had his books, had no longer
to worry about "his two old arch-enemies, time and money,"
and had not Mary to bother him, Richardson tells us—in four
paragraphs (pp. 167–71)—what he read, the progress of his
thinking up to this time, and the effect the new writings had on
him. And while Mahony's philosophy of existence occupies four
paragraphs of summary, Mary's pregnancy takes up four pages
of summary narration. Such a narrative summary is structured
around ideas, rather than scenic action. The first paragraph of
this sequence, for example, tells of Mahony's bewilderment, dis-
may, and his feeling of inadequacy at the prospect of having
children at his age; the paragraph also provides a summary of

the Mahonys' desire over the years to have children. The next paragraph discusses the "good side" of having children now that they have the money; and the third deals with the question of providing a nursery for the child. The last paragraph describes Mary's condition throughout her pregnancy.

Richardson's use of block description, while valuable, is rarely accompanied by a balanced amount of dialogue and action. The description of Buddlecombe, for example, seems weighty in relationship to the rest of the chapter, which develops the scenes of Mary and Richard at breakfast, and Richard on his morning rounds. Not only is Buddlecombe described as it looks but it is described as it looks at the time Richardson is writing the novel. Richardson makes no attempt to conceal this; she explicitly says that "nowadays, its streets go everywhere up and down."[26] Why a description of the town as it appears in the present is more important than developing characters in the context of the specific setting is a puzzling question.

But Henry Handel Richardson does this elsewhere: her descriptions of Mrs. Turnham's house, the Mahonys' house in Melbourne, and in the last volume, the house in Hawthorn, are presented as she visited them at the time she was writing the novel. There seems to be no artistic reason for this use of the block description of settings, other than to remind the reader that Richard Mahony was drawn from a character who actually lived. Because she is forced to cover so much material, it would seem that she should consider this material irrelevant in the face of the more important considerations of a scenic style.

Style, however, as a primary consideration does reveal itself in Richardson's use of the interior monologue. While this technique becomes a major part of the last volume of the trilogy, its beginning comes toward the end of *The Way Home*. The method is crude, even in *Ultima Thule*; nevertheless, it is an attempt to mold events from the viewpoint of Cuffy Mahony, through imposing his expressions, interests, and reactions on those events. When Richard and Mary leave to attend Tilly's marriage for example, Richardson presents the events from the eyes of Cuffy. She begins to spell words as Cuffy would say them, such as "hi-spy-hi" and "pitchnick," in an attempt to reflect the nature of his thinking process. This technique represents a rudimentary form of the interior monologue that becomes increasingly important as the trilogy progresses. It will provide, as well, for an additional method of presenting the meanings of the trilogy through the eyes of a small boy.

While it is used only rarely in *The Way Home*, the interior monologue is one of the most effective vehicles for meaning in the novel. Meaning in *The Way Home* is limited primarily to Mahony's continued questioning about the nature of existence; his inability to find a true home in England, Australia, or Europe; and Mary's gradual realization that "amid life's ups and downs, to be able to keep one's little flock about one, to know one's dearest human relationships safe and unharmed, was in good truth, all that signified." The recurrent imagery of confinement and escape is illustrated, as I have indicated, by Richard's restless movement from the confinement of a dirty manufacturing town to a coastal town; from the confinement of Buddlecombe's society of values based on background and manners to the wealthy Melbourne society; and from the confinement of the gaudy luxury of the squatter society to the more genuine splendor of the Continent. Mahony's feeling of confinement, as has been stated, by way of various fancies and physical discomforts, takes him from city to city on the Continent, until he is forced to return to Australia. His escape from confinement, as in *Australia Felix*, is always physical escape; but its satisfaction is brief and the desire to seek a new physical environment is ready at hand, always demanding satisfaction. In *The Way Home*, this craving grows more intense as the book progresses, even as the needs of food, shelter, and luxuries are fulfilled beyond expectation. The culmination of this restlessness is the trip across the Continent.

And just as Mahony's restlessness grows, so does Mary's impatience. By the end of the book, she is willing to agree that practical and common sense considerations are not everything; but her impatience with Richard's illogical approach to life makes her assert her will more often as the events of the book progress. Her comment to Richard, as they arrive in Melbourne with the knowledge of their fortune, is as central to the thematic base of the book as her final realization that she must rely on the human relationships of her family. She tells Richard he tires easily of things; and such a comment is symbolic of the nature of their changing relationship. Richard needs care as her children need care; and while Mary has been gaining steadily in strength and stature, Richard has been, as Mary comments about his physical appearance, "growing down."

XIII   Ultima Thule:
Summary and General Critical Analysis

The last volume of *The Fortunes of Richard Mahony*, published in 1929, follows Mahony through his return from England to his death in Gymgurra. At Barambogie, just before he attempts suicide, he realizes that "the plain-truth was: the life instinct had been too strong for him. Rather than face death and the death-fear, in an attempt to flee the unfleeable, he had thrown every other consideration to the winds, and ridden tantivy into the unknown."[27]

Henry Handel Richardson's presentation of the events of the book is broadly based on the three-part structural framework: Mahony's return to Australia until his child's death in Barambogie; the falling-off of his Barambogie practice up to the point when he decides to move to Shortlands Bluff; and the difficulties of his practice in Shortlands Bluff until his death in Gymgurra. All three parts of the structure indicate three major stages in Mahony's final years of life.

The structural pattern of *Ultima Thule* appears to be more dramatic than panoramic. When Mahony returns alone to Australia, for instance, the focus of the structure is on his actions and thoughts rather than on the Melbourne of the 1870s. Mahony's very actions dictate a structure that will show his family in isolation—dramatically portrayed, as if under a microscope. His depression over his lost fortune makes him follow a course of behavior that ends in total isolation.

Richard's attempts to settle financial matters without contacting either his Melbourne or Ballarat friends constitute a well-placed clue to the novel's total structure. Such a course of action forces the narrative to examine the restless, impractical direction of his thoughts and actions, which are due in part to his desire to circumvent Mary's criticism of his decisions. When Mary and the children arrive, the narrative takes in their thoughts but rarely broadens to include a picture of the society. We are quickly introduced to Mary's actions and thoughts through her conversations with Richard, and with Cuffy's thoughts and point of view toward the events of the plot. But the sphere of activity, again, is limited to the activities and people in the new house at Hawthorn. Even Mary's attempt to broaden their friendships is thwarted; and she finally decides to have friends in when Richard is away.

The other events and settings of *Ultima Thule* seem to reinforce such a dramatic unity. While *Australia Felix* and *The Way Home* concerned themselves with the crowded *dramatis personae* of Ballarat during the gold rush, English manufacturing-town and coastal-town society, and wealthy Melbourne society, the last volume of the trilogy makes little attempt to portray the people of Hawthorn, Barambogie, Shortlands Bluff, or even Gymgurra. The pattern follows the events in Richard's mind, rather than the characters and characteristics of a society. Instead of placing Richard in a panoramic context, *Ultima Thule* stresses his single, dramatic struggle to retain his sanity and avoid poverty. The characters around him are only useful insofar as they reflect the activities of his mind and throw up barriers before him. Any interest we have in the societies of the "bush" country of Australia is superseded by our concern for Richard's dilemma. While Richardson had available a colorful and adventurous panorama—the rugged outback towns of the early 1870s—she never makes use of it in the way she describes Buddlecombe or the wealth of Melbourne.

The events in Hawthorn, as in Barambogie, are representative of Richardson's use of a few characters. While Mary carries on activities with old friends and a few new ones, Richard, in center focus, does not. Probably the best example occurs during a birthday party Mary has arranged for her children. The birthday party is going on at full swing as Richard sits in his surgery, isolated, pondering the hundreds of pounds he is in debt. His pride had made him neglect to tell Mary of their financial position, and this is one of the things that drives him into isolation, even from his family.

In Barambogie, the structural framework becomes even more dramatic. Instead of describing the town and people of Barambogie, Richardson introduces the setting through a series of letters Richard writes to Mary, while looking over the prospects of the practice. The reader's picture of the setting, then, is exclusively through Richard's eyes—his initial reactions, his doubts, his optimism, and his final decision to make the move. Along with Richard's viewpoint, the reader is aware of Mary's reactions to her husband's letters, since each of the letters begins with Mahony's attempts to reply to his wife's letters. Both these viewpoints are central throughout the Barambogie sequence, and they are essential to an understanding of the dramatic structural framework. Even before he goes to Barambogie, Mahony's characterization guides the course of the structure by a further desire for isolation.

In Barambogie, more than in any of the other settings in *Ultima Thule*, it becomes clear to what extent Richard's characterization and the dramatic structural pattern are fused. Richard's desire for isolation and the resulting focus on Richard and the family instead of on characters in the context of a panoramic structure, seem to form the total underpinning of the novel. The "small shop-keepers and farmers, and vine growers, and licensed publicans" of the town are rarely presented in any detail.

Other indications of the dramatic nature of the structure come after Lallie's death, when Richard remains with the practice at Barambogie while Mary and the children spend a few weeks vacationing on the coast. Mahony's feeling of sorrow is translated into a spiritualistic reunion with his daughter, coupled with an initial feeling of satisfaction that he is able to isolate himself even from Mary and the other two children. His need to isolate himself even from his family is a further indication of the direction his characterization takes.

The culmination of Mahony's desire for isolation at Barambogie comes with the threat of a lawsuit for malpractice. Even the circumstances surrounding the case that nearly brings on the malpractice suit indicate such a desire. After the case is brought to light, and the patient is sent to Oakworth hospital, Richard is forced to wait several days to hear if his mistake can be corrected. It is at this time that he attempts the ultimate in isolation—suicide.

The move from Barambogie to Shortlands Bluff, while not directly the result of Mahony's attempt to isolate himself, is necessary if Richard is at all interested in earning a living. The people of Barambogie have rejected him; he must move on to another practice and isolate himself, in a sense, among other townspeople. As in Barambogie, Shortlands Bluff and its people are never described; only a few patients and neighbors are portrayed as they relate to the events of Richard's life. But Mahony's continual interest in privacy provides further clues to the limited number of characters in the last volume. When he rows out to inspect a ship in his capacity as acting health officer, for example, he is possessed by the need for keeping his eyes averted from the view of others.

While separate instances concerning the children and Mary provide the occasion for the introduction of more characters— such as the acquaintance with the Spence family, Purdy's visit, and Tilly's visit—Mahony's concern for isolation continues to be both an isolation from the society of Shortlands Bluff and the members of his own family. The culmination of his desire for isolation comes with Mary's decision to take in boarders; but it is no ordinary desire. The structural pattern after this time remains dramatic, and focuses chiefly on the other members of the family—particularly Mary and Cuffy. At Shortlands Bluff, however, Richard makes his last bid for privacy before insanity blacks out his mind forever.

XIV   Ultima Thule: *The Use of Dream Sequences*

The focus of narration in *Ultima Thule*, like the structure, is more intensely on Richard Mahony than in any other volume of the trilogy. Perhaps the best example of Richardson's use of point of view in *Ultima Thule* is her depiction of Mahony's dreams. In this last volume, Mahony has a dream of extended length and concentration in Barambogie, after he is threatened with a lawsuit for malpractice. This lengthy and complex dream, which becomes a nightmare for Richard, anticipates the trial for malpractice by placing him in a courtroom faced by his accusers.

The dream exemplifies Richardson's continual focus on Mahony's mind. It makes no attempt to place Mahony, as the instrument of the dream, in the narration; as he is reflected in the past and present of his life, he is portrayed only as he appears in the context of the dream. The only outside agent in the course of the dream sequence is Mary, who attempts to wake her husband, as the dream itself ends. The dream moves the reader, with no introduction, into Mahony's mind.

The point of view shifts, quite effectively, from Mahony's attempts to escape those who in the dream have accused him of malpractice to his attempts to escape his wife, who tried to wake him. So, too, does the narration shift from the world of the dream to the conditions of the present. The past and present events of Mahony's life have been filtered through the viewpoint of the dream just as they have to a more limited extent in the other scenes of the novel.

XV Ultima Thule: *Multiple Viewpoints*

The framework of the proemlike first chapter of *Ultima Thule* introduces other aspects of point of view. Mahony's decision to start a practice in Hawthorn and build a house is compressed into a five-page summary. With the arrival of Mary and the children, six months later, the actual scene of arrival is described in full detail. The transitional shift into the next chapter comes with the family awakening in the new house several weeks later; the point of view, however, is Richard's. Through both the first and second chapters, Richard's mind is the vehicle for events in the immediate past. A jump forward in time is often made from the end of one chapter to the beginning of the next, but the events are always presented during the course of the next chapter—and most often through Richard's consciousness. In chapter two, for example, Mahony lies in bed remembering how his wife reacted to their house weeks earlier and what she did during the course of those weeks.

After enough of the past events are filtered through Richard's mind to make the present events understandable, a complete scene in the present is described. Chapter 2, for example, which shows a family breakfast, describes conditions such as the noise of the children, which Richard still has not gotten used to after several weeks of living in the new house. As a result, the effects of previous events, which have not been described, are brought into the present without transitions. The narrative continues to inform the reader of minor happenings and incidents in the interim while, at the same time, the action of the scene is progressing. Such a technique is used throughout *Ultima Thule*; chapter 10 of part two, for example, ends with Mary's hopes for Richard in Shortlands Bluff.

Chapter 1 of part three begins with Mahony in the thick of his job at Shortlands Bluff, several months later, as seen first from the viewpoint of Cuffy and then Mahony. Mahony's comment on his condition at Shortlands Bluff fills in the details of the past few months, and the details of past events are again brought into the present without transitions. Mahony's growing physical difficulties are described in the perspective of his difficulties at Barambogie. The events of the plot unfold rapidly, and the reader is supplied with the necessary background detail of past events to insure the proper emphasis. In nearly every case the events are filtered through Mahony's mind.

XVI Ultima Thule: *Major Characterization*

Characterization in *Ultima Thule* is closely tied to the use of dramatic structure and limited third-person point of view. Both the structure and the characterization of Mahony are connected to Richardson's purpose; she is concerned with portraying increasingly greater degrees of isolation. The ultimate in isolation is the blocking off of the mind from the real world; and in Mahony, this is achieved through complete insanity. But the point of view, as well as the structure, contributes significantly to this characterization. By concentrating on Mahony's limited point of view of events, and even his interior responses, Richardson is able to show increasing degrees of isolation more effectively.

Built around the framework of isolation and alienation, Mahony's characterization centers on the two basic elements first introduced in *Australia Felix*: his conflict with Mary's commonsense ideology and his continual questions about the nature of existence. Both aspects are either revealed or solved before Mahony's death; and the process of revealing and solving expands Mahony's character considerably. We learn, for example, that his conflict with his wife has always thwarted his sense of freedom, and that his attempts to escape physically by moving to England, Barambogie, and Shortlands Bluff are also, in part, moves to escape from the philosophy of life represented by his wife. The culmination of this sense of thwarting comes as insanity overtakes him, but it is best represented in the dream he has when threatened with a lawsuit for malpractice. At the end of the dream, while escaping from his accusers, he is stopped by Mary; and he reacts by attempting to stab her.

Such intense feelings toward Mary indicate the course their relationship has taken. The culmination of this relationship is reflected in Richard's last sane act—the burning of his business documents. "At the sight of her standing in the doorway," he attempts to "shake his fist at her," to "hurl a scurrilous word," to "spit at her in vain." Even earlier in the trilogy, during his attempted suicide, it is Mary he rails at; she gives way before his greater instinct of self-preservation as do the children.

While Mary takes on symbolic value for Richard, as the embodiment of all the money-grabbing, opportunistic people he has fought against for so long, his attempted suicide takes on greater meaning. Mahony finally understands that the answer to his questions of man and existence is suffering, not escape from suffering. He casts away the phial of poison, unable to complete the task. Although brief, this one moment of perception brings Mahony at last to an understanding about his relationship to the universe. Although it comes too late for him to pattern his life around it, such an understanding does make him realize that he must take a less taxing job at Shortlands Bluff in order to attempt to regain his health. The state of his physical and mental health, nevertheless, cannot be repaired; and Mary is the last person to understand just how ill her husband has become.

The differences between Richard and Mary appear to form the essential structure of *Ultima Thule*. As Richard becomes insane, he attacks her practical sense of things by setting fire to the hated business documents. But Mary moves away from her commonsense, practical view of life as the book progresses. At the end of *The Way Home*, she had begun to conclude that sorrow and waste occurred everywhere and were unexplainable. And with this understanding, in *Ultima Thule* she is forced to alter her attitude toward life, to understand the narrowness of the purely practical approach, and to recognize this fact of man's exposure to care and suffering.

Mary is probably most thoroughly convinced of suffering after Mahony's collapse, when she must take the job of postmistress with all of its worries. She not only assumes many of Richard's nervous obsessions about the job, but she realizes that the purely practical approach does not save her from the cruelties of a day-to-day strain. Her change of attitude is best illustrated when she does everything to bring Richard home from the public asylum. Before this, she had used her customary, commonsense approach by agreeing to have Richard transferred from a private hospital that she could no longer afford to the state asylum. But Mary's ideas of care and suffering have brought out qualities never before present—imagination and a love that sweeps away the practical for the fanciful and foolish. When she visits the state asylum, she becomes convinced that he must be released. She finds that he is refusing to eat his meals because they are served on tin plates. She defends Richard to the warden, saying "all he needs is to be treated like a gentleman . . . by gentlemen!"

Mary has clearly changed in her consuming interest in the practical; she understands Richard's needs for eating on "crockery," respects them, and defends them in much the same way Richard would have defended his idiosyncrasy. She now disregards the warden's concern for the practical—the tin dishware—whereas before she would have at least partly approved of such a measure.

And after this time, she seems to be constantly aware of the power of the imagination. The most striking example of this is her appeal to Henry Ocock's imagination and memory, when she does everything in her power to convince him to have Richard released. The chance that she might lose her job, that she might not be able to handle him, that the children might be upset by him—all these contingencies would have brought nagging doubts to such a plan before. She is consumed with a love born of suffering and is determined, as Richard always was, that one must do everything to adjust one's behavior to the realization that man is more than an animal. But her love and imagination, ironically, come too late; Richard is unable to benefit by it. We have the vague feeling that Mary's talents for love have been wasted because her "practical-sense blindness" to Mahony's condition caused her to withhold her understanding and sympathy.

She is not, as Richardson hints, a woman who has carried out "a lifetime of unwearied sacrifice" for her husband; she has simply misunderstood him and placed all her cares on the practical considerations of money. She has lost much of life's meaning in her misinterpretation of God and man's suffering, just as Richard loses in his concern for a Hereafter, before the cruel realities of everyday life. Although she matures, she matures too late to help Richard, and as a result they remain conflicting personalities never completely reconciled. Richardson has put the necessity of suffering into two intensely universal characters and shown their development in the context of suffering.

XVII   Ultima Thule: *Minor Characterization*

The minor characters of *Ultima Thule* are effective static and inflexible "flat" characters. Agnes, Purdy, and Henry Ocock remain as they were originally portrayed in *Australia Felix*, as do the other characters from the Mahonys' Ballarat and Melbourne days. There is, of course, the emergence of Cuffy as an important minor character and commentator on the later events of the book, and perhaps it is his characterization, together with that of the bishop and Baron von Krause, which is most representative of Richardson's best minor characterization in *Ultima Thule*.

The bishop, a picture of the rugged, optimistic colonial in *Australia Felix* and *The Way Home*, visits the Mahonys in Barambogie just before Richard's attempted suicide. He is first pictured as he was—a "genial, courtly gentleman." After observing him for a few days, however, Mary realizes something about his character she had never noticed before; and through her realization, we begin to perceive an interesting new side to the bishop's optimism. First, Mary notices that he consoles Zara about her husband's death in the same manner and with the same words he used in consoling her about her own daughter's death. Such a revelation, coming as it does at the lowest point in Mahony's life, not only provides a contrast with Richard's way of dealing with suffering but shows another way of avoiding reality through an insensitive approach to death.

Baron von Krause's portrayal, on the other hand, appears to reflect Cuffy's characterization as the bishop's reflected Mahony's. During the course of the baron's visit to Barambogie, he discovers Cuffy's innate talent for music and suggests that Cuffy study music in Germany. His characterization and actions during the course of his stay reveal both the ignorance of Mary's commonsense approach to music and Mahony's sensibilities—in short, the conflict between the two major characters which forms the centerpoint of the trilogy. When the baron realizes that Cuffy has musical talent, he encourages him to write music about the new, rugged terrain of Australia. While the idea of musical study is thwarted by Mary, the baron's praise strengthens Cuffy's character and makes us realize that the potential lost in Mahony might be regained in his son.

As a character, Cuffy retains his childlike fears and concerns; and his distinctive quality appears to be his musical talent. A more unusual picture of Cuffy occurs on the many walks he is forced to take with his father, just before and after Mahony's mental breakdown. While Cuffy's reaction is an effective part of his characterization, his reaction to his father's insanity is interesting for its impressions on the boy's personality and later development. Cuffy's fear of being laughed at before the rest of society, coupled with his sensitivity, is a child's fear of being labeled out of the ordinary. Richardson's description of Cuffy during Mahony's funeral illustrates Cuffy's attempts to "wall" himself "up against unhappiness." It also parallels Richardson's description of her last visit to the graveyard of her father—a determination to be happy set against relief.

Richardson uses minor characters to serve as reflectors of the major characters; and Cuffy, while an effective flat char-

acterization, is a flat character attempting to become round.
The perspective Cuffy gives, through the possibilities of his
musical talent and his view of the final events of the book,
together with his relationship to the baron, show a roundness
that only hints at its full potential.

XVIII   Ultima Thule:
Plotting, Proem and the Use of Dream

Other plotting devices, while in some ways similar to those
of the first two volumes, represent interesting variations. The
use of the proem in *Ultima Thule*, for example, is distinctly
varied; instead of making use of an opening chapter entitled
"Proem," Richardson places all her introductory, thematic, and
symbolic material in the first chapter, along with the scenic
events of the family's arrival from Europe. And while it is not
formally prefaced by a proem, the first chapter of part one
indicates the state of Mahony's life up to the time he returns
to Australia. The proem to *Australia Felix* pictured the people
of the vast gold-rush era of the 1850s; and the proem to *The
Way Home* portrayed the colonial returning home after a life
in the colonies. The material that introduces the reader to
Ultima Thule describes the plight of the alienated colonial, who
has tried both sides of the world and knows no home. Since
he has established no roots, he can only yearn for one country
while inhabiting another. It is left to a later generation, hopefully
Mahony's children, to know Australia as "home."

The framework of the first chapter introduces other plotting
devices in *Ultima Thule*. The interplay of character in action,
for example, is a significant plotting technique; in this novel,
it dictates a specific chain of circumstances set by the decisions
that Mahony has made. The basic action forces Mahony to
make choices that trap him in a series of circumstances leading
to his death. He loses his fortune, for example, after he has
lived a life of luxury for nearly ten years; and this fact contributes to his decision to build a large house when he returns
to Melbourne nearly penniless. The debt on the house, together
with the inadequate income earned from his Melbourne-Haw-
thorn practice, makes him decide to move to Barambogie. At

Barambogie he hopes to earn enough to pay off the debt, but his daughter's death and his unpopularity render him unable to meet the payments. At the same time, his earlier illness with sunstroke in Ballarat recurs, forcing him to seek a less taxing practice in Shortlands Bluff. At Shortlands Bluff his growing illness becomes both physical and mental, until he can no longer stand the pressure of his financial obligations. In each case, Mahony is compelled to act by the specific circumstances of his environment and of his physical and mental condition. The point of origin is his pride, based on a wealthy past, which makes him spend money needlessly in Hawthorn, before his wife and children arrive. All else follows from this first moment of pride.

This interplay of character and action, decision and circumstance, is enhanced by still another plotting device: foreshadowing. Foreshadowing assumes a pattern of unity which links earlier characters, situations, and incidents to later ones for thematic effect. The most outstanding instance of foreshadowing in *Ultima Thule* is the dream at Barambogie. We have mentioned this dream because it reveals a special point of view; as an instance of foreshadowing, it is just as important in revealing the unity of the entire trilogy. The specifics of the courtroom scene can be traced back to his early life, as a storekeeper in Ballarat and a doctor in Buddlecombe. As a storekeeper, he had been taken to court by a man called Bolliver because he refused to pay for goods lost in transit. Just as Bolliver lost the case many years earlier and was ruined, so now does Mahony lose the case in his dream and find himself ruined. But, as he sits in the courtroom, he also finds a messy conglomerate of melting jujubes in his pocket and is forced to move to the opposite side to escape the sticky mess, just as he was forced to return to Australia when he heard Mrs. Saxeby-Corbett criticize his wife's colonial manners, during a brief moment while Colonel Barker, a guest of the Saxeby-Corbetts at Buddlecombe Hall, found that "he had left his jujubes in the pocket of his greatcoat."[28]

After Richard reseats himself on the other side of the room, the dream begins to narrow to its climax; he discovers why he is in court, who the plaintiff's counsel is, and who the defendant is. In trying to discover who the plaintiff's counsel is, Richard draws from two sources of memory: Bolliver's counsel and his old friend Purdy. When Richard begins to realize that "everyone present was more or less familiar to him," he recalls images that only the reader can identify as being relevant to his past life.

Both Bolliver's counsel and Purdy are part of Richard's depiction of the lawyer who is arguing the case against him. The plaintiff's counsel seems to be a picture of both Mahony and the man who plans to accuse Mahony of malpractice. Such a plaintiff is, of course, not the Mahony of the Bolliver trial but the Mahony who is struck with the physical disease that causes paralysis of the legs, a poor sense of coordination, and lapses in speaking. This disease appears to resemble drunkenness and is taken as such by the townspeople of Barambogie, who have observed Mahony's stumbling, incoherent sentences as he introduced an old Ballarat friend, Archbishop Long. Mahony's appearance of drunkenness is also referred to when he is accused of malpractice; he is called "a damned, drunken old swine" by the would-be plaintiff, who has seen him around town and observed what appeared to be drunkenness in his manner.

Just as the plaintiff physically resembles Mahony, so does the defendant. But this time the dream identifies the defendant openly as Mahony, and he becomes the focus of the trial, both as defendant and spectator. The defendant who enters the witness box resembles both Tangye and Bolliver in appearance. Tangye is described as a "tall, haggard-looking fellow whose muscles on his neck stood out like those of a skinny old horse"; he is "old, and grey, and down-at-heel fifty, if a day—and his clothes hung loose on his bony frame." When Richard meets Tangye in Ballarat, he remembers how Tangye looked to the townspeople: "Though not a confirmed drunkard, he had been seen to stagger in the street, and be unable to answer when spoken to."[29] Ironically, Tangye's condition appears to be that of Richard's position in Barambogie; they have both been afflicted with diseases that induce a drunkenlike state through paralysis and loss of memory. Richardson has shown, then, through portraying the plaintiff as drunk, that the drunkenlike state has surrounded Mahony throughout his life—even during his prosperous years in Ballarat, when he confronts an image of his older self in the embittered chemist Tangye. Tangye was probably accused unjustly in Ballarat as Mahony was in Barambogie; and Richardson has undoubtedly used Tangye in the first volume as a foreshadowing of Mahony's breakdown as it is seen in the last volume.

The Mahony in the dream—Mahony the spectator—realizes how others view him for the first time when he sees the face of the defendant as his own face, and he nearly utters what is to become an archetypal "insane scream." The reference to the shriek is another of Richardson's intricate and effective projections into the future, since, when Mahony goes completely mad, he believes that he has uttered an insane scream which shatters all the boundaries of the real, sane world around him. The fear of such a scream has been voiced before the dream, when Mahony sits in his surgery at Barambogie. After Mary has taken a vacation on the coast, he waits for patients and the nerve-wracking sound of the mill whistle, until he is almost certain self-control will be lost, forcing the utterance of the terrifying, insane scream.

Mahony must do nothing else but escape from the conditions of the dream. And this is particularly clever foreshadowing, for escape has been Mahony's way of dealing with a problem all his life. But the escape of the dream is as difficult and as ineffective as have been his escapes in life. In the dream, his escape only leads him to impossible frustrations.

The focus shifts from the defendant to Mahony the spectator, who struggles to escape down an endless row of seats crowded with people whose legs are slowly paralyzing into immobility. His terror-stricken movements are reminiscent of the theme of chase and hunt that runs throughout the trilogy. Perhaps the most relevant parallel is the pathetic chase and hunt of Long Jim in the proem to *Australia Felix,* for Mahony has definitely replaced Long Jim in that symbolic scene at the opening of the trilogy. Richardson has clearly intended Jim's desperate run from the license hunters in the Ballarat gold diggings to parallel Mahony's headlong run toward annihilation.

Mahony's "running like a hare": and the "knife concealed" are the keys to the foreshadowing that this part of the dream so effectively develops. "Hare imagery" is reminiscent of Bolliver's pet rabbits whose throats he slits after learning that he has lost the lawsuit. The knife that he uses to slit the throats is Mahony's "knife concealed"; and, just as Bolliver kills those things dearest to him, Mahony attempts to kill his family because they have thwarted him. This feeling of being thwarted by his family runs throughout the book. Even in the earlier parts of the trilogy, during his attempted suicide, it is Mary he rails at; she gives way before his greater instinct of self-preservation, as do the children. This is foreshadowed by his speech of questioning that begins: "*Were* they dearer?"

The total dream, from the first scene in the courtroom to Mahony's wild attempts to escape his wife and his attackers, reveals an employment of foreshadowing that ranges over all the earlier events of Richard Mahony's life. We see now the reasons for the detailed analysis of Bolliver's trial in *Australia Felix*, for Mahony's long conversation with Tangye after a successful party, and for the scene at Mrs. Saxeby-Corbett's, when Richard learns that his wife is being rejected because of her colonial manners. Even Mahony's attempts to escape his wife's practical demands on his time are illustrated by his attempt to stab her at the end of the dream.

XIX Ultima Thule: *Setting*

The four major settings of *Ultima Thule*—Hawthorn, Barambogie, Shortlands Bluff, and Gymgurra—reflect increasing degrees of the tightening family unit, from Mahony's desire for alienation, isolation, and privacy to Mary's determination to have Richard with the rest of the family even in helpless insanity. Each of the four towns is described only as it relates to the Mahony family unit. While each of them takes something from Richard, they also take things from other members of the family and from the family as a whole. Hawthorn takes money that turns into a house they cannot afford and an insurmountable debt; Barambogie takes both a daughter from the family and Mahony's professional and emotional pride; and Shortlands Bluff takes Mahony's sanity. It is only left for Gymgurra to take Richard's life; and just as the family must leave Lallie's grave behind in Barambogie, they must leave Mahony's behind in Gymgurra. Each of the environments contributes to the degeneration of the family unit; and each serves as an environmental force, tearing down Mahony further—in a sense readying him for insanity and death.

While Shortlands Bluff does lead to the asylum, Mahony's underestimating his condition indicates the power of the environmental force dragging him down. Just as this last volume describes all the outback towns and forgotten holes of colonial Australia, it also describes the power of this force to destroy a man. Put together, Barambogie, Shortlands Bluff and Gymgurra show aspects of the ruined man, the person who did not make it in Australia and yet is forced to disintegrate and die there. Hawthorn is a more prosperous town, and Shortlands Bluff even a kind of winter resort, but the Mahonys feel unwanted there, and Barambogie and Gymgurra are unquestionably the symbols of ruined men.

Other examples of ruined men that reflect Mahony's plight appear in Barambogie and contribute to the setting. There is, for example, Reverend Thistlethwaite, who is made a definite part of the setting of this town that eventually makes Mahony attempt suicide. Mary's survey of the town reveals a number of characters who reflect their own plight. The description of Gymgurra, where Richard is to die, becomes a further indication of the environmental forces that conspire to break apart the family and bring about their ruin.

XX   Ultima Thule: *Theme*

Richardson projects her meaning through the use of several thematic passages on the nature of Mahony's life, struggles, and death. Meaning in *Ultima Thule* is primarily limited to Mahony's brief discovery of the answer to his questions about the nature of existence, Mary's complete realization that the strength of the family unit and the understanding of man's condition of suffering takes precedence over practical success, and Australia's final "absorption" of Richard's body and spirit as his final and eternal home. The most significant part of these is Mahony's understanding that the answer to his questions of man and existence is suffering, not escape from suffering. After attempting to commit suicide at Barambogie, Mahony casts away the phial of poison, unable to complete the task. He learns that pain is the bond that links humanity and that "not in joy, in sorrow alone were we yoke-fellows."

A second lesson, which occurs as Richard mulls over his financial problems after his daughter's death in Barambogie, crystallizes the recurrent imagery of confinement and escape, of the hunted and the hunter. It is not only the imagery of the hunt and the hunted, but also the theme of annihilation in wild attempts to escape the reality of death. The concluding passage of the book extends this theme even further: as Henry Handel Richardson reflects upon Richard's grave, she reveals the final peace of his existence.

Mahony's death becomes his ultimate peace, and ultimate answer to the questions of existence. His knowledge of suffering as the link that binds all men is fused, by death, with his submission to man's mortality. But Henry Handel Richardson's choice of an epitaph for *Ultima Thule* signifies another aspect of her theme. By choosing the same quotation from Ecclesiasticus (44: 90) that Hardy uses in *Jude the Obscure,* Henry Handel Richardson suggests a theme of wasted and unfulfilled humanity. This theme is perhaps best indicated by the starkly depressing aspect of Mahony's last years. His life appears to have no justification, even though he learns that his bond with humanity is his suffering. And yet Richardson tells us: " *'And some there be, which have no memorial. . . .'*"

CHAPTER 6

Henry Handel Richardson as a Short Story Writer

I Summary

*T*he *End of a Childhood* (1934), Henry Handel Richardson's book of collected short stories, contains work published between *The Fortunes of Richard Mahony* and *The Young Cosima*, and it includes an earlier story, "Death," retitled "Mary Christina" for the collection. Two other stories, "The Coat" and "Sister Ann," remain uncollected and will be discussed separately.

The collection begins and ends with two deaths. It opens with the death of Mary Mahony in "End of a Childhood: Four Further Chapters in the Life of Cuffy Mahony," an extension of *The Fortunes of Richard Mahony*, and closes with the death of Mary Christina in a story drawn from notes on the death of the author's mother. While much of the first story comes from the mind of Cuffy Mahony, his mother's perspective on death is clearly similar to Mary Christina's.

Other clues to the unity of the volume come in the center sections. "Growing Pains" follows Cuffy Mahony's story, and traces the insecurities, trivial tragedies, and awkwardnesses that follow initiation into adulthood. Part two includes "Life and Death of Peterle Lüthy" and "The Professor's Experiment"—both harsh accounts of adulthood in the naturalistic vein. The final story, before "Mary Christina"—"Succedaneum"—outlines Richardson's view of the artist as both above society and escaping from it by withdrawing into the tower of art. Green calls it "Richardson's most explicit statement of the value she placed on art as a refuge from unhappiness" and the "converse of the attitude in 'Mary Christina.'"[1]

II *Literary Analysis*

The story "The End of a Childhood," subtitled "Four Further Chapters in the Life of Cuffy Mahony," is linked with the final chapters of *Ultima Thule*. Mary lies awake in bed, worrying over what might happen to her orphaned children if she died. It is also linked with Cuffy's childhood fears that now without a father, and then just maybe without a mother, he might be left completely alone. The four chapters, then, outline Mary Mahony's death and Cuffy's final realization, in the smell of wattles, that his new life alone carries hope and possibility. The symbolic wattles bring to mind the wedding journey of Cuffy's parents from Geelong to Ballarat, years earlier, and as a result guarantee that the strengths and weaknesses in the boy include resilience and the will to live.[2]

Other events sum up the character of Mary and foreshadow the accident that will bring about her death. She refuses Henry Ocock's offer of marriage with the pride that was her husband's and is now hers. Instead, she begins to whitewash the house in preparation for a journey to Melbourne to look after Cuffy's education. Her fall from the ladder results in a broken leg that will not heal. She puts off a trip to the hospital as long as possible, again adopting Richard's pride and determination to be self-sufficient. And before she is forced to leave for the hospital, Mary begins to ask the very questions of existence that filled much of Richard's intellectual life.[3]

First, she questions existence itself—a motif repeated in "Mary Christina." Next, she questions the nature of her own actions in the scheme of life but is unable to admit their limitations—which ultimately becomes the extroverted, "plain thinking" mind unable to cope with the abstract. Her answer tends to vacillate between accepting things as they are and continually repeating the question "But *why* was I made like it? Who's responsible?"[4] As Mary Mahony leaves, on a stretcher improvised from Cuffy's bedroom door, the two children display antithetical feelings about their new independence, and they experience a vague excitement. The former, quite naturally, is the stronger emotion, and since the chapters are told for the most part through Cuffy's mind, it is his confused sorting out of events that records the action:

So he played alone. Just at first Mamm's going left a sort of hole in him (like the door). But after that he thought he was really rather glad. For when she wasn't there he didn't need to think so much about her. She wasn't *nice* to think of, since she fell off the steps—not able to walk properly, and her face was so red and swollen. He wanted her to look like she always had.[5]

Aunt Tilly, a longtime friend of the family, returns to tell the children that their mother has died and they must be separated. As Aunt Tilly prepares the furniture for sale, Cuffy rebels against the concept of change on a child's level much in the same way as his mother questioned existence, his father resisted it, and each of the other characters in Richardson's novels confronted most of the ramifications of its meaning. And Cuffy questions, as well, why as a young man, he cannot have a say in the decision making when Jerry and Tilly sort out their finances and arrive at a solution. It is decided, since Uncle Jerry cannot afford to keep both children, that Cuffy must go with Tilly. This decision makes Cuffy assert his mother's wish that he take care of Luce "no matter what," and, while he loses his wish that they grow up together, his initiation into manhood is complete when his concern for her welfare becomes more important than his own desire to be comforted by her presence: "She was most dreadfully afraid of horses; and it gave him a pain right through him only to look at her and think how afraid she was."[6] Cuffy's final gesture—the burial of the pocketknife his mother had given him for his birthday—reinforces a growing conscience. It also recalls the burial of Lallie, in Barambogie, and of Richard at Koroit. Immediately after he smells the wattles, which is a recurring image in the trilogy, Richardson tells us that "Mile after mile combined to stretch the gulf, that would henceforth yawn between what he had been, and what he was to be."[7]

Part two, "Sketches of Girlhood," contrasts Cuffy's growing maturity with stories of all children's growing tragic awareness of the disenchantment and transience of love. As Richardson portrays male and female relationships, she seems to indicate again and again that men and women occupy societies closed to one another. While Cuffy understands the nature of familial love, Laura, in *The Getting of Wisdom*, like the adolescents

Nell and Peggy in "Preliminary Canter," experiences disappointments. "And Women Must Weep" intensifies the theme of communication breakdown, as does "The Wrong Turning"—a dramatic, painful sketch of a young boy and girl who go boating only to find themselves alongside a camp of soldiers, bathing in the nude. Romanticism and realism seem to clash head on as the two grope toward love—a theme familiar to most of Richardson's works, and central to *Maurice Guest*: "Something catastrophic had happened, rudely shattering their frail, young dreams; breaking down his boyish privacy, pitching her headlong into a reality for which she was in no wise prepared."[8]

While "The Wrong Turning" employs more of the drama and tension of a short story, pieces like "The Bathe," subtitled "The Grotesque" and "The Bath," subtitled "An Aquarelle," are often pieces Laura might have written after her school days— "fragments, decorations chipped after some larger structure."[9] They possess valuable thematic material dealing with the transience of beauty, which Richardson sees as so important to Laura's final revelation in *The Getting of Wisdom*. In this way they are certainly of value as thematic links. And like the others they do fit within the book's structural pattern. The first is a six-year-old's vision of two aging ladies who decide to follow her example and bathe in the nude on an isolated beach. The ladies serve as a painful initiation as they undress:

So this was what was underneath! Skirts and petticoats down, she saw the laps that were really legs; while the soft, and cozy place you put your head on, when you were tired. . . . And suddenly she turned tail and ran back to the pool. She didn't want to see.[10]

And as they came out of the water to dry off, the horrified "Laura" sees them ". . . as they lay there on their sides, with the supreme mass of hip and buttock arching in the air, their contours were those of seals—great mother-seals come lolliping out of the water to lie about the sand."[11] The child's final response is even more direct than Laura's flight from school: "Oh, never . . . never . . . no, not ever now did she want to grow up. *She* would always stay a little girl."[12]

The second sketch, "The Bath," serves as the lyrical opposite.

It celebrates the beauty of four preadolescent girls bathing, and, while the moment is permanent and held in time, the sketch's conclusion rests with a similar defeat of beauty: "the splashed walls and swimming floor drained dry; the bath-water gurgled off; and the mirror's surface lay blank, no conjurer being at hand to call to life the lovely shapes that slumbered in its depth."[13]

"Two Hanged Women," the story that ends "Sketches of a Girlhood," reemphasizes Laura's pattern of dependence between a younger and older girl. But the older girl, Betty, unlike Evelyn, serves as a continuing mother figure to the younger girl. In fact, she encourages the role and sides with her friend's terror of being pushed into a marriage she detests. There seems, then, to be no reasonable acceptance of sexual roles. The female in society cannot, ultimately, adjust to anything resembling a normal relationship. Instead of anticipation there is always ugliness and repulsion. "And Women Must Weep" sums up the dilemma of boy-girl relationships. A young girl, Dolly, is attending her first ball. To her disappointment, and through the pressure of her Aunt Cha, she discovers that no boy will dance with her; she returns home early, a failure. Her reactions sum up the painful and the impossible: ". . . For really, truly, right deep down in her, she hadn't wanted 'the gentlemen' any more than they'd wanted her."[14]

Part two, "Two Tales of Old Strasbourg," deals with the oppressive ends of lives, whereas "Girlhood Sketches" had surveyed youthful disillusionment and emotional abnormality. "The Life and Death of Peterle Lüthy" concerns the death of an illegitimate child from cholera. The mother, indifferent to Peterle, leaves him alone while she goes dancing with her stepfather. As the baby's illness grows worse, the reader's awareness of adult shallowness increases—a man dying from consumption in the same apartment house, who is jealous of the living; implied incest between Henriette and her stepfather; and the atmosphere of indifference that pervades the people of Strasbourg, including the Italian whom Henriette befriends at the dance and the vegetable-hawker who lives in the attic. All seem to live in a naturalistic world that they have neither the initiative or the ability to control. Even the doctor who attends the child allows Henriette to take Peterle away when it is clear he needs hospitalization, and when she takes the baby to the hospital, all the doctor says is: "Why come here only when the child is dying?"[15] Even the doctor who signs the death certificate stays afterward to crack jokes and drink wine with the family; and the coffin maker, instead of making a real coffin, substitutes a balcony box he needed to get rid of.

Henriette's walk to the cemetery, pushing the perambulator with the dead Peterle in his green box, becomes a set piece in Zolaesque naturalism. Few who see her pass know what is in the green box, and the baby is lowered and covered quickly, after which she stops at a pavement café to drink a glass of beer, and then dozes off to sleep in the summer sun.

The second story of Strasbourg, ironically entitled "The Professor's Experiment," is in contrast to the first. The first story finds death to be a commonplace; the second finds it to be an evasion of life. The "experiment" of the professor is to marry late in life despite the objections of his eldest sister, Annemarie, who has cared for him like an indulgent wife and resents the intrusion of a rival. But the professor's wife, Elsa, instead makes Annemarie aware of her brother's petty, narrow mind, which concerns itself more with the mystery of his Oscan Declension than human life. Elsa's personal habits, tastes in books, and lively personality—"the fine inborn gaiety of her nature"[16]—begin to decline from day to day. Elsa sees their life as a collection of "doll-like gestures," from the formal greetings, to the professor's friends, to the monotony of the day to day routine. Since she is displaced in the house by Annemarie, Elsa is never allowed to minister to her husband's needs. She quickly sees that her own friends, and even the wives of other professors, are not welcome in the house. Rapidly, "the Professor seemed to her a mere dry little pedant, without a single human stirring under his hard-baked surface" and "Before Annemarie, she stood the eternal school girl in face of her mistress."[17]

The prospect of birth alters Elsa's frustration and supplies both the professor and Annemarie with a focus for Elsa's "purpose" in the household. When Elsa's father dies, the disruption takes on almost catastrophic proportions, since he was Elsa's only link with the freer society outside the confining rigidity of the professor's household. After a rest at a watering place in the mountains, Elsa still seems to be declining in health, and the doctor raises still another question—whether her basic constitution is suitable for child-rearing. With the birth of the child, the professor's world collapses around him; within the "delicious" prospect of correcting proofs for his latest publication comes the birth of his child and the night afterward the death of his wife; then a fortnight later, the death of his child. Only for a brief moment does he show genuine emotion; the rest is for his *role* as a poor widower.

Annemarie progresses, on the other hand, toward a transformation. She rejects her routine—the one she has sustained for the past twenty-five years—and becomes filled with fear at the silence of the house: "the mysteries of birth and death had been enacted before her: the coming of a new soul, the going forth of one with whom you had shared your daily bread. This was life—what it really meant to be alive—not the humdrum monotony that had always fallen to her lot." The result of her awakening is a rejection of the professor and all he stands for.

"The Professor's Experiment," clearly one of Richardson's best stories, develops a strong sense of two characters who have evaded life and of one who sees the shallowness of this invasion in a striking and carefully foreshadowed resolution. Like "Peterle Lüthy," there is a death of a child, but the consequences are totally different. The first story has the quality of a set piece, while Annemarie's conversion and the careful, convincing picture of the professor as pedant makes the story rise above its naturalistic roots.

"Succedaneum," the next story, is weaker as fiction than it is as Richardson's statement on art, life, and the terror an artist feels when his inspiration has failed him. Both Green and Kramer suggest that this should be read as an autobiographical statement, since Henry Handel Richardson herself was between books, literarily barren, and fearful of symbolic desertion that would come with the death of her husband as it came years earlier with the death of her father.[18]

Jerome Moçs, the central character, is about to finish his most important symphonic work when self-doubt stops him. With this comes a feeling of separation—from society, his fellow artists, his art. Each quality is important to the central characters of Richardson's novels in one form or another. Moçs becomes fascinated with the poster of a singer called Bianca, and pursues her throughout Europe without success. He focuses on her eyes, a familiar enough motif in *Maurice Guest* and the trilogy. He finds, instead, a substitute in Salli. He educates her on the model of his imagined woman but later discovers her as a real, lovable woman in her own unshaped form. She becomes his shadow, as the earlier title of the story, "Shadow and Substance," indicates more directly—the symbol of his own, limited, earthly self, " 'the mute shadow at his heels' which he cannot escape to find the true incorporeal soul." Eventually he discovers that Bianca, the singer, is in the neighborhood and meets her, only to find her a grotesque caricature of what he had imagined, only her voice left intact and "ideal." He leaves her for a train ride back to his Salli, but on the journey, discovers that "the gift of creation was his again, he was one with his daemon, his genius; with that mystic force which justified his existence" and he regains "the handful of notes, the combination of tones, needed to start the chain of ideas that should carry him rapturously to the end."[19]

After some hesitation, he telegraphs Salli: "Am not coming back. Return home." Ironically, only when Moçs has truly loved does he find himself able to open up to his art. As Green indicates, he must learn "to love both the substance and the shadow."[20] Space symbolism, so skillfully used in the trilogy to describe Mahony's growing madness, is used here to dramatize walls that blocked Moçs. Moçs' realization that he has gone from a metaphoric summer idyll of "sleep" to an "awakening" as he meets his ideal in the flesh also appears in the trilogy, but there it has slightly grimmer conclusions. Life, rather than a summer of love, is sleep, whereas death is a confrontation of the great awakening.

"Mary Christina," the last story of the volume, describes the physical sensations of a woman dying in great pain. First published under the title "Death" in 1911,[21] it was then reprinted as "Mary Christina," together with "The Life and Death of Peterle Lüthy," in 1931,[22] under the title *Two Studies.* As a part of *Two Studies*, it emphasizes in point of view and theme the

contrast between Peterle's inability to articulate his pain and
Henriette's indifference to the death of her child. And as the
last story in *The End of a Childhood*, it compares the imaginary
account of the mother's death with the real one. Mary Christina,
like Niels but unlike Mary Mahony, dies the skeptic, refusing
hope in immortality or even hope in a few more minutes of life.

Hopelessness in "Mary Christina" is symbolized in the form
of circles of pain. She feels caught in a Dante-like whirlpool
which leads to a certain agonizing darkness. After this, her body
would be poised in a center in the horrors "of the dark," and
she would hear the waters meet, as if she were poised on a
spit in the bottom of the ocean, "with a crash of thunder, above
her head." As the pain increases, she is beyond responding to
it. The "waves have rushed over her head"; she is "without
substance, without meaning, it had all been an idle beating
of the air."[23] Arriving at a point of complete nihilism, she
unravels the last particle of hope, and the rest is simply physical
reaction to the moment of dying. Only the observer of the
event, not Mary herself, sees the thoughts of the dying woman
fuse essence with mind: "Now, she asked for rest—only for
rest. Not immortality: no fresh existence, to be endured and
fought out in some new shadowland, among unquiet spirits."[24]
She dies, by her own wish, unblessed. The denial is complete;
"Mary Christina," as the last story of *The End of a Childhood*,
replaces the affirmation of "Succedaneum" with a complexly
developed denial of immortality.

And finally, even the last scene itself—the observer's perspective—reinforces Mary Christina's nihilistic position:

The black-robed woman who remained, raked out the embers of
the fire, and pushed back the chairs from the bed. On the eyes of the
thing that had been Mary Christina, she laid two squares of damped
muslin; and, as she did so, she made fervid intercession with
the other Mary—the Gracious Namesake of this poor soul that had
gone unblessed into the darkness. The covering decently stretched
and folded, she turned out the gas, and set a nightlight in a glass
of water.—It threw living shadows on the wall.[25]

By contrast, the only thing living is the *shadow* of the night light, composed of water, a life-giver, and glass, its fragile container.[26]

T. H. Lawrence's critique of this story in a 1932 letter to Jacob Schwartz indicates some revealing comments about the story's strengths and their relationship to Henry Handel Richardson as a novelist.[27] He writes that "parts of her Australian trilogy were quite careless, as prose..." but "she has lavished great pains upon these two stories ('Death' and 'The Life and Death of Peterle Lüthy,' as they appeared in *Two Studies*)."[28] While he notes six instances of stylistic difficulties in "Mary Christina," he concludes that "if she could write a book like this it would beat her Thule books out of court, fine and large though they were."[29] The stylistic difficulties, noted after an unusually perceptive examination of the story, include the use of cliché, borrowed influences, discordant prose rhythm, one question of punctuation, one of syntax, and one concerning a minor plot discrepancy. But most are single instances, and most argue for, rather than against, Richardson's ability to write excellent short fiction.

Even a superficial glance at the critical positions on Richardson's short stories, with the exception of Dorothy Green's, shows that Richardson "is not a distinguished practitioner of the art of the short story."[30] Another comment, certainly not unusual, tells us that "*The End of a Childhood*...is hardly worth critical discussion since it is so plainly marginal to her achievement."[31] While her novels, as Lawrence affirms, have the advantage of "largeness" of character, structure, and setting, what can the polished style of "Mary Christina" tell us about her novels? Lawrence seems to have pointed to one of the most critical issues in the works of Henry Handel Richardson, and he provides the reader with some tentative conclusions. For all the criticism about Richardson's prose style, it is clear, in his analysis, that not only was she capable of writing excellent short fiction but of writing polished, undeniably skillful prose.

III Uncollected Short Stories

Of Richardson's last two uncollected stories, "The Coat"[32] and "Sister Ann,"[33] "The Coat" exhibits her ability to examine the psychological and spiritual inwardness of an apparently realistic encounter. Two women meet for lunch and a shopping expedition in London, and after lunch one of them is hit and killed by a bus. Instead of using the omniscient point of view, Richardson uses the selective omniscient which becomes the voice of Katherine in a state of semiconsciousness as she is dying in the hopital. What unravels is the story of Katherine's failed attempts to impress Margaret that her life has been happy, her marriage a success, and her husband, Harry, a man in an important job. The controlling symbol for these fantasies is Katharine's fur coat, which she has purchased by stealing money from her husband's meager savings. Dorothy Green contends that the theme of the coat is drawn from spiritualistic belief. It concerns "the gradual disengagement of the soul from its two envelopes: the outer garment, gross matter, what we are accustomed to call 'the body,' and the second garment, or *perisprit*; this also detaches itself from the body and follows the soul, 'which thus finds itself always clothed in a garment.' "[34] Since the coat becomes Katherine's false outer garment, she is asked to shed it—first by a man, then by her dead mother, who persuades her to confess the lies she has told Margaret to protect herself from the truth of a shabby, deceitful marriage. But this has only been done *after* she has removed the coat—in a sense removed both the "body" and corrected the earlier lies of *perisprit*. The steps in this process can be found in *The Evidences of Spiritualism,* an account probably available to Richardson through her studies of her father's papers for the trilogy.[35] For some people, as for Katherine, who have become absorbed in material pleasures, release of the symbolic "coat" will become more difficult. In fact, the *perisprit* has become identified so closely with the coat that it becomes a kind of "skin," only to come off painfully and laboriously. As her mother urges her to "hurry" in releasing the bonds uniting the soul and the body, she knows Katherine must not only remove the coat but tell the truth before disengagement is complete. The humming of the "dead" becomes deafening when she refuses to talk. When Katherine does, she still needs a "mantle" to hide behind, and this becomes, ironically, her mother's dress, with which she covers her face as she speaks her confession. And still she clings to one sleeve of the coat as she attempts to follow her mother's vanishing form.

The story ends in the hospital, and as Margaret meets Harry— "a shabby, careworn little man, of the sloping shoulders and limp, uncertain movements."[36] The garbled last words of Katherine, together with Margaret's impression of Harry, corrects the image of her dead friend's life until "deeply pitying, believed she understood."[37]

"Sister Ann," quite unlike any of the stories in *The End of a Childhood*, carries some of the affirmative tone of Mary Mahony's voice in *Australia Felix*. Sister Ann, the eldest of seven girls, is forced to operate a ranch completely on her own. While the daughters are motherless, their father, who bought the land on the rumor that it had gold on it, is left helpless before the responsibilities of a squatter's ranch, and he carries himself through by getting drunk daily on rum. It is left to Ann to see after the "hands, horses, stocks," and to prod her sisters into helping with some of the necessary work on the farm. It is also her responsibility to find suitors for each of the girls, and she demands that her sisters press their suits with the hope that one of them will marry a wealthy squatter who will in turn support the rest of them.

After a number of false starts, Ann discovers a wealthy squatter called MacNab and forces Gemma, "the beauty of the family," to court him, but Gemma does so without success. To Ann's surprise, it is she whom he asks to marry. At the same time, she discovers that her sisters resent her pushing and wish to be left alone to make their own mistakes and to seek their own lives independently of her. This is reinforced when MacNab offers to give her father a loan, to help the station prosper, and tells her he has seen the sisters' need for independence from the beginning. Slowly, but effectively, MacNab persuades Ann. The other sisters, who watch the courting process, already begin to assert themselves. Just as Ann accepts the proposal, Gemma is figuring out ways to lure another suitor—one that Ann thought was unsuitable for her.

Richardson's ability to make a situation dramatic with skillful insight into human interrelationships surprises us. MacNab is developed as insightful, sympathetic, and perceptive—quite the opposite of the Devines in the trilogy or the scores of "ignorant squatter" patients Mahony tends in the course of his career. Rather than the painful incompatibility of sexual relationships outlined in "Sketches of Girlhood," there is a perfect fusion of personality between male and female. As MacNab says, and Ann finally sees, they are "people who're labouring for the same end. And to whom work's a sort of gospel."[38] The difficulty of courtship and the painful denials of a girl rejected at her first ball in "And Women Must Weep" contrast sharply with the compatibility of a man and a woman in "Sister Ann." As Gemma plans to lure back her "tall, dark, handsome lover" at the story's end, still another example of a congenial relationship is hinted at and, as a result, runs counter to the painful, hopeless "growing pains" and portrayal of sexual abnormalities in *The End of a Childhood*. Published posthumously, "Sister Ann," while not a great story, clearly shows a psychological shift in Richardson's somber vision (often called an Anglo-Australian one) of the Australian experience.

CHAPTER 7

The Young Cosima

I *Summary and Preliminary Analysis*

The Young Cosima (1939), Richardson's last novel, reconstructs the marriage of Cosima Liszt to Hans von Bülow and her rejection of him for Richard Wagner. The book opens in Berlin with von Bülow's confession of love for Cosima and devotion to the musical genius of her father, Franz Liszt. Liszt has placed Cosima in the care of Hans's mother in Berlin, and Cosima is determined that she will marry Hans, against his mother's wishes and to her father's amazement.

From the beginning, her life's desire is music, and her talent grows into dedicating herself to the man who is endowed with the divine gift of creating music. She becomes a good housewife for Hans precisely because it is clear that, without distractions, Hans can become a composer of genius. Cosima gradually discovers, however, that Hans is a slave to Wagner and to the interpretation of his music. By becoming a fervid admirer and promoter of Wagner, he destroys his own talent and chances for a career.

At first, Cosima reacts angrily to Wagner, and continues to carry out a schedule of daily self-sacrifice to Hans. But as the months pass, she begins to realize that ". . . he couldn't persuade himself to dodge an appointment or leave a friend's errand undone. . . . And over these and similar things he wore himself to shreds."[1] She also begins to realize that Hans might be only "a dry husk if it were not for the vitality that Wagner's genius pours into him."[2]

As Cosima's dislike turns to admiration, she defends a critic of *Tristan and Isolde* after Wagner gives a reading of his masterpiece. She concludes that Hans will always remain a disciple and interpreter, never a creator. And after Wagner's separation from his wife, Minna, Cosima begins what becomes a courtship of admiration for the spirited, impish, eternally young personality of Richard Wagner. To her, Wagner becomes the genius of personality and music that represents the heights of the creator.

Wagner, now under the patronage of King Ludwig, invites Hans and his family to stay with him for the summer. Burdened with work, Hans sends Cosima and the children ahead of him, unaware that he has given Cosima and Wagner time to seal their love. A letter sent to Cosima by Wagner, some months later, falls into Hans's possession, and he goes to Triebschen to confront Wagner. Ironically, Wagner successfully diverts his anger: "with the manuscript of *Meistersinger* open before him ... the musician in him utterly routed the man...."[3] Hans, as Cosima has concluded, is torn between Wagner's genius and needs on the one hand and his love and desperate need for his wife on the other. And yet he can evaluate the man correctly when he says to Cosima: "Your standards are ... so high; and in him, out of his genius, is so much that is only ... clay."[4] Like Schilsky, Wagner's genius rests above society's conventions. And like Louise, Cosima is intent on loving the highest order of genius and disregarding its amorality. But Cosima is less "possessed" than Louise and perhaps more consciously calculating and intellectually aware of her decisions. Above all, it is the *work* of art, now standing apart from the artist, that needs to be completed— in this case the *Meistersinger* and later *Tristan*.

And now the irony of the relationships between Hans, Wagner, and Cosima becomes immense. Cosima has genuine sympathy, concern, and love for both Wagner and Hans. Just as she felt impelled to maintain a smoothly running household for Hans to create in, she feels even more impelled to do the same for Wagner. And yet, she discovers, Wagner *feeds* on Hans's ability to perform the Master's work: "the one needs the other equally: composer and conductor needed to think and feel as one and meanwhile a labor of every contact."[5] This is further complicated by Ludwig's growing knowledge of the affair between Wagner and Cosima, which could lead to a loss of patronage. But Wagner, breaking with society's conventions, demands that Cosima divorce Hans to be with him, and he rationalizes it by

believing that his only wish is that she should no longer suffer
the gossip, personal slights, and affronts brought on by their
affair! Again, as with Hans, he wins her consent through the
greatness of his own music—his appeal to Cosima's desire that
Siegfried be finished.

Returning to Hans, Cosima confronts him with her decision
to stay with Wagner permanently, to turn Protestant, and to ask
for her release. While Cosima bases her decision on the greatness of Wagner's art, both husband and wife sort out the factors
that led to this separation. Hans, in encouraging his wife to
love the genius of Wagner, further led her to love the man. Her
love for genius in the abstract becomes her concern: which of
the two men needs the greatest emotional support in order to
create? And yet Hans's evaluation of the nature of Wagner's
needs seems embarrassingly accurate:

"Of course, he needs you. . . . There's never been a time when
he hasn't needed—someone! And now more than ever: to share his
exile, take the edge off his loneliness, soothe the tantrum his un-
natural life engenders. But *any* woman by nature fool or saint enough
to fall in love with his whims would do equally well. . . . the chapter
of Richard Wagner's *amours* is not one I'd care to read to any woman;
but his you can take to me: it isn't *in* him to be faithful. His heart
is like his genius, perpetually in renewal. No more to be relied upon
than a rope of sand."[6]

Hans also reminds Cosima that she must secure the consent
of her father, who has devoted his last years to Catholicism. This
results in a final interview between Hans and Wagner, after
which Cosima is instructed by Wagner "to bend that 'wild-bull
Hans'" to the Wagnerian will.

Hans agrees only to arrange a meeting with Cosima's father,
with the stipulation that her presence with Wagner in Triebschen
be kept a secret. His anger never allows them to touch; yet if
they had just "met hands," the rapid course of events might have
have been altered. Cosima, while still certain that the highest
service is to the greatest artist, cries as she leaves: "'Oh Hans,
my poor, poor husband, what am I doing to you.'"[7] Richardson
describes her leaving "Pale, trembling, exhausted; but unshrink-

ing. For she had heard what she believed to be a 'call'; had found her lifework. And whether she went towards it in joy or pain was not hers to decide."[8] She creeps out of the house at dusk, "like a thief on a journey."[9] And yet art is a destiny, like faith, and she has committed herself to the crucible of genius. *Siegfried* must be finished.

II   *Critical Analysis*

While *The Young Cosima* is set in the world of music, its concern from the outset is the complex emotional relationship between Hans von Bülow, Cosima Liszt, and Richard Wagner. In her letter of December 5, 1938, to Nettie Palmer, Henry Handel Richardson asserts that "it is not a musical novel. Only about those whose trade music was."[10] And in a letter writtten on May 6, 1939, she reinforces this: "... it was the relationship of the people that interested me most; not the woman's career."[11] As Green indicates, it is Henry Handel Richardson's most penetrating analysis of character interrelationships to be found in any of her novels.[12] But even more important, it is the author's attempt to *understand* the motives that sustained the relationships between Liszt, Wagner, Bülow and Cosima, not to justify one of the relationships in terms of the morality of art.[13] Professor Kramer writes that the novel shows a "preoccupation with the artist's role, and with the inner forces that bring a man to success, and whose absence spells artistic and personal failure."[14] This most recently published statement (1971) on *The Young Cosima* is supported by other evidence.[15]

Green's and Kramer's statements appear to take distinctly different positions on the novel. While the letters as cited indicate that relationships and motives are most important to *The Young Cosima*, such a statement does not imply that relationships need to be as broadly defined as Green maintains or so narrowly delineated as Kramer seems to suggest. Henry Handel Richardson's interest, surely, was in motivation and relationships, but she was interested in this particular story precisely *because* it was about a subject to which she had devoted lifelong study and thought, namely, music. As Olga Roncoroni says, Richardson was disappointed in the reviews of this last novel because the critics were unwilling to admit that Wagner was a man who often spoke and wrote letters like the average mortal.[16] She had been interested in portraying a musician accurately from historical sources, had done so, and yet was criticized for making a musical genius talk like a comman man. This seems to indicate that while relationships were her primary concern, a lifetime of writing about the artist (or would-be artist, as in the characters of Richard Mahony and Laura) and lifetime involvement in music made a realistic novelist like Richardson instinctively turn to music for her materials. Further verification comes from Arnold Gyde, an editor at Heinemann who sent Richardson a manuscript collection of Wagner's letters, suggesting that she might want to use them in one of her future projects.[17] While his assumption was that she would write a "quick" book, her interest in *both* the subject and the personalities and their relationships led to collecting and reading a hundred volumes on the topic and spending a number of years in research and composition. The artist, his music, and his life entanglements seem, then, to form the core of this important last novel. All are of importance in evaluating Henry Handel Richardson's contribution to the art of the novel.

Three themes stand out as crucial to Richardson's interpretation of Cosima Liszt: self-sacrifice, love, and genius. Whether these are viewed as central or secondary to Cosima's need for a Wagnerian father figure to provide her with "creative offspring" after his death is still another question.

III *Use of Historical Materials*

The historical materials leading to an interpretation of the three themes consist of primary sources (chiefly letters by and to the Wagner family and telling the story), secondary sources (the voluminous correspondence and the numerous biographies of Wagner, as well as Hans von Bülow's letters and contemporary accounts of him) and miscellaneous information concerning men and music of the time.[18] Not only was Richardson a collector of a library of Wagneriana, mostly in German, with marginal notes in her own handwriting, but her mind was also a storehouse of memories of musicians and musical training from her years in

Leipzig. She was also, of course, author of a novel involving a careful study of musicians in the context of their human interactions. All this contributed to the making of *The Young Cosima*.

Since Richardson limits herself to the period between the courtship and marriage of Cosima to Hans von Bülow and the last few hours with him before she leaves permanently for Wagner, the author works "on a small canvas but with essential absorption of detail."[19] This covers a little more than a decade of Wagner's life—roughly the period between 1857 and 1868.

Sometime during 1857 Wagner moved into a garden pavilion called *Das Asyl* ("The Refuge"), built by patron friends, the Wesendonks, in Zürich. Cosima joined Wagner in the autumn of 1868, but they were not married until 1870. During this second period of Wagner's career, Richardson reveals the artist's greatest phases. The composition of *Tristan und Isolde,* permeated with tragic irony as each emotional incident is defined by the evolving musical phases of an irresistible love, is followed by his comic drama in music, *Die Meistersinger*. Just as *Tristan* dramatizes his outer life with Cosima, *Die Meistersinger* becomes a defense both of the artist under attack and of the genius of the folk, which Wagner claimed was the source and core of modern art. And finally comes the composition of *The Ring*, in which he comes to grips with materialistic civilization.

Amid the creation of this art stands the maturing, self-possessed Cosima, who through a decade's time is portrayed by Richardson as a strong, determined sacrificial heroine of great art. She is "ultra-modern"; she sees the human side of great art. And even more than Wagner, she possesses patience, diplomacy, and tact, sacrificing everything for her lifework. But it becomes clear that Wagner also attracts Cosima because he satisfies her need for a father, and a promoter of his art after his death.[20] Evidence abounds to show that she is most concerned about preserving the work of art itself, at times more so than the creator himself. This process, as Green defines it, fulfills her own creative drive. When Wagner proposes to Cosima that they go away and live together in Paris, her response is conclusive proof that she puts the creation of art over love itself:

"A mansarde in Paris, eh, Cosel? You and I alone together, subsisting somehow, living only for each other and our happiness. Come, what about it?" By now she was crying in earnest. Yet staunchly she shook her head. "Die Meistersinger," she whispered.[21]

Since Wagner is the father-genius who replaces Liszt, it is also the dedication to self-sacrifice learned as a child that makes Cosima see the two as fused. She talks this over with her sister Blandine early in the story:

"Do you remember a sermon we once heard preached by Abbé Gabriel? . . . Well, in it he said that the life of a true woman ought to consist wholly of self-sacrifice, she herself stands for the 'sacrificial offering.' I never forgot that; the words seemed to burn themselves into me. At the time it was Papa I dreamed of dedicating myself to. Now I know Papa doesn't need me; but poor Hans does; and if I can help him and through him the greatest of all Causes—why, it seems to be a chance I dare not miss."[22]

Other sources reinforce this—Liszt's last visit to Cosima and their early Mass prayers together, which produces a "mystical" union; Liszt's approval of her marriage to Hans and Wagner's offhanded comment when the two girls are young: "So, from now on, I will be your *lieber Papa*." Wagner's direct identification with "love," "father," and "daughter" when he meets Liszt and his daughter are still other indications of his future role of both father and lover to Cosima. This becomes an identifiable symbolic scene as Cosima grows a little older. Liszt returns to Germany after a long absence, and the meeting between the three becomes an embrace that turns into a physical union: "they stood, the three of them, linked as one, she and her two dearest." And again, the identification of the father, lover, and child becomes clear in the later scene in which Liszt accompanies on the piano Richard's singing of *Die Meistersinger,* while Cosima thinks: ". . . not only had she succeeded in bringing back to Richard the friend she had given up for lost. But, in that outer room, genius sat by genius. . . . Oh, that the stimulus of Liszt's presence might inspire him to take up afresh and bring to an end this glorious, all too long neglected work!"[23] Cosima, as Richardson interprets her, takes what at first seems to be the feminine role of self-sacrifice. But this is combined with what is defined in contemporary times as the masculine creative drive, which is drawn, the writer shows, from Cosima's need to identify with the more visible father.

IV   Structure

Cosima's father, Franz Liszt, seems to be the structural center of the complex web of relationships of Bülow, Cosima, and Wagner. All three are emotionally attached to him, and yet he enjoys a certain detachment from each. As Richardson indicates, Bülow's closest attachments are with Liszt and then Wagner, while he often views Cosima in a brotherly fashion. His discovery of her love letters to Wagner produces fear of Cosima's strength over the Master, and, oddly enough, sexual jealousy. It disturbs him "that her strength" trespass on Wagner's essential masculinity (synonymous with his creativity), which Bülow regards as accessible only to him.[24]

The other interrelationships center around Richardson's use of the structural pattern of an opera in three acts. It rests, according to one critic, in the first act on Bülow's "passionate (and unsuccessful) desire to have Liszt for a father by marrying Cosima."[25] The scenes follow in this manner: Bülow and Liszt; Liszt and the Princess (the "sacrificial victim"); Liszt and Cosima (the "sacrificial victim"); Cosima and Bülow; Frau von Bülow and Liszt (the mother and the father); and Cosima and Bülow. Wagner, on the other hand, is only heard off-stage. The second act identifies Hans with *Tristan* rather than Cosima. At this point the *Tristan* "poison" begins to take effect, only to envelop Cosima in the third act. The third act is climaxed by the reunion of Wagner and Liszt and the triumphant performance of *Die Meistersinger*—all described from the point of view of Cosima. The Tristan music is replaced by *Die Meistersinger* in this act, rounding off the operatic structure.

V   The Young Cosima *as Richardson's Last Novel*

Henry Handel Richardson was nearly seventy when *The Young Cosima* was published in 1939. Her husband's death had profoundly influenced her personal and writing life. She, as well, was drawing for the first time on purely historical materials and was undoubtedly more interested in the situation of the characters than in the implications of its history. Each of her other novels can be traced back to autobiographical sources. All these factors contribute to the problem of language and narrator.

While the *New York Times Book Review* for August 10, 1969, praises *The Young Cosima* over a more recent biography of Cosima,[26] most critics comment upon its heavy use of cliché, its overwritten quality, its impatience and "feverish" prose style, and the confusion of the language of the narrator and the characters.[27] The book became a burden to her, whatever the source. The insight into the characters' relationships to each other, rather than the characters themselves, remains her primary contribution in this last, painstakingly written novel.

CHAPTER 8

Conclusions

WHILE Henry Handel Richardson will always be recognized for the range of her influence and for her conscientious realism in the early *Maurice Guest*, her power to develop convincing central characters within the boundaries of the realistic method remains her chief contribution to Australian fiction. Richard Mahony, in *Ultima Thule*, will probably stand as the best example of her genius. While she counts *The Getting of Wisdom* as her favorite book, it remains by comparison a brilliant, compact but limited development of adolescent character. *Maurice Guest*, "invading pre-war England" with a narrative technique based on European models, stands next to *Ultima Thule* and means much to the later English fiction it influences. She was the first Australian novelist to develop a central character study in depth. As early proof of what was to emerge, her proem to *Australia Felix*, which foreshadows the tragic course of Mahony's life and thus embodies the entire structure of the trilogy, remains her best prose writing.

The publication of Dorothy Green's *Ulysses Bound* in 1973 marked a major shift in the course of Richardson criticism since it began in earnest after Richardson's death. While in 1960 Cecil Hadgraft was quick to call Richardson "by common consent our greatest novelist,"[1] her writing was attacked for its "literal mindedness" and its clumsiness of style as early as 1954.[2] This took on the form of a "school," as Dorothy Green indicates, with the publication of several books or pamphlet-length critical studies designed for large, general audiences. These are principally Vincent Buckley's *Henry Handel Richardson* (for the Australian Writers and their Work series) in 1961, Leonie Kramer's study (for Oxford University Press's Great Australians Series in 1967, which had worldwide distribution), and Profes-

140

sor Kramer's 1971 introduction to the Penguin edition of *The Fortunes of Richard Mahony*. While other critical positions were taken during this period,[3] most were limited to periodical publications with small readerships. Even before World War II Richardson was labeled a naturalist when naturalism was out of favor, and her books were held up as examples of the failure of the naturalistic method;[4] and after the War she was called a chronicler who displayed little imagination but an abundant command of the facts. Green's thesis, in her exhaustively comprehensive *Ulysses Bound*, is that Richardson was an imaginative novelist, not a mere chronicler, and that her work can be read on many levels, including the psychological, the moral, the mythic, and the literal. Even more important is this critic's determination to shift current literary opinion, principally the widespread judgment set by Kramer and Buckley.

But the argument, and its implications, becomes enormously more complex and important than this. When asked about the differences between their positions, Professor Kramer said in an interview that her argument with Dorothy Green was not about Henry Handel Richardson but about the limitations of the realistic method.[5] Dorothy Green's response was: "I do not know what Professor Kramer means by the 'limits of realism.' The limits of any art form are determined by the skill of the artist using the form."[6] But Green, Kramer continues, is proving that Richardson departed from her realistic materials to prove that she transcended them to become a great artist. Only *The Getting of Wisdom*, which she draws on heavily, yields such proof.[7] However, Green responds again: "Arguments about realism, naturalism, expressionism etc. etc. always seem to me to interest critics more than artists. Real artists use them all just as the need occurs, as far as one can define any of them at all. What is the story of the Good Samaritan? Purely naturalism—one *fact* stated after another—yet it all amounts to a tremendous symbol. Sorry about this—but I'm so tired of the whole theory!"[8] Professor Buckley, while not concerning himself with Kramer's line of argument, simply admits that, after a careful look at the Richardson papers deposited in the National Library in Canberra, he would have undoubtedly revised his opinion on literal-mindedness. And since he considers *Ultima Thule* her best book, he would have written at greater length, as well, on its excellence of writing.[9] In short, he agrees with Green that a careful examination of the Richardson papers would probably reveal a more imaginative and less literal-minded writer.

Finally, we are left with the statement of Professor C. B. Christesen, Richardson scholar and longtime editor of *Meanjin Quarterly*, that "Richardson criticism begins with Dorothy Green's book, *Ulysses Bound*."[10] While *Ulysses Bound* is certainly the most comprehensive study of the life and personality of Richardson, as Elizabeth Loder claims in her review in *Southerly*, its extensive examination of Richardson's life and work is descriptive criticism rather than evaluative.[11] We are left with the impressions that Richardson has indeed transformed her materials and is indeed imaginative rather than literal-minded, but we are less satisfied with Green's discussion of literary achievement. Some of the attention to individual works is determined more by their value for the study of Richardson's life and psyche than by their literary merit. This is certainly true, and yet much that is discussed is specifically labeled as descriptive to place Richardson's work within a philosophical context in Western intellectual history. The evaluation of *Maurice Guest* as an examination into the nature of love and of the trilogy as centering on the relationship between father and mother, as revealed by the Neustatter papers, is especially instructive.

Dorothy Green's vision of Henry Handel Richardson bound to the mast of her work beckons us to follow, if we are willing to take the care that an examination and appreciation of Richardson's work demands. Until more fiction has been written, her reputation as the finest Australian realist will stand.

Notes and References

Chapter One

1. In her autobiography, *Myself When Young* (London, 1950), she gives the address as 1 Blanche Terrace, whereas her most recent and most comprehensive critic-biographer, Dorothy Green, in *Ulysses Bound* (Canberra, 1973), p. 22, gives it as "Blance Terrace (i.e., 139 Victoria Parade)." Since so many of the facts of her life have been incorrectly quoted, the following information has been verified by Mrs. Green and Olga Roncoroni, her literary executrix, and the information in the Australian National Library in Canberra. Any errors that exist in this account are not the result of my sources of information, but my own inabilities.

2. Henry Handel Richardson, *Myself When Young* (London, 1950), pp. 1–2.

3. See the papers of Walter Lindesay Richardson in National Library, particularly the following notebooks and account books: MS 133/32, 35, 36, 37, 38 and Alan Stoller and R. H. Emmerson, "The Fortunes of Walter Lindesay Richardson," *Meanjin Quarterly* 29, no. 1 (Autumn, 1970) 32.

4. Alan Stoller and R. Emmerson, "Richard Mahony, Walter Lindesay Richardson, and Spirochaete," *Henry Handel Richardson 1870–1946*; papers presented at a centenary seminar (Canberra, 1972), p. 9.

5. M. A. Clutton-Brock, "The Melancholy Optimist: An Account of Walter Lindesay Richardson and His Family," *Meanjin Quarterly* 29, no. 2 (1970), 193.

6. Henry Handel Richardson, *The Way Home* (London, 1930), p. 455.

7. Dorothy Green, "Walter Lindesay Richardson: the Man, the Portrait, and the Artist," *Meanjin Quarterly* 29, no. 1 (Winter, 1970), 7.

8. F. B. Smith, "Spiritualism in Victoria in the Nineteenth Century," *Journal of Religious History* vol. 3 (Spring, 1965), 254.

9. Stoller and Emmerson, "Richard Mahony, Walter Lindesay Richardson, and the Spirochaete," p. 10.

10. Clutton-Brock, p. 195.

11. Richardson, *Myself When Young*, p. 4.

12. Leonie Kramer, *A Companion to 'Australia Felix'* (Melbourne, 1962), p. 19. Kramer notes that the marriage in the trilogy takes place in the spring of 1854, probably to include the fictional Mahony in the Eureka Stockade. Such a fusion of the history of the Ballarat goldfields would allow for Henry Handel Richardson's latitude with the facts of her father's life while maintaining historical accuracy.

13. Richardson, *Myself When Young*, p. 4.

14. Register of Midwifery Cases, Ms. 133/24, National Library, Canberra.

15. F. B. Smith, "Spiritualism in Victoria in the Nineteenth Century," p. 254. (See also Dr. Smith's account of Dr. Richardson's significant contribution to the Victorian Spiritualist Movement in *Free-Thought in Victoria in the 19th Century* (Canberra, 1960).

16. Stoller and Emmerson, "Richard Mahony, Walter Lindesay Richardson, and the Spirochaete," p. 12.

17. Walter Lindesay Richardson Notebooks, Ms. 133/36, National Library, Canberra.

18. Richardson, *Myself When Young*, p. 5.

19. Olga M. Roncoroni, "Main Facts in the Life of Ethel Florence Lindesay Richardson," Ms. 133/80, Box 11, the Australian National Library, Canberra. This is the latest, most accurate account. A more complete bibliography appears at the back of the book. Portions of her autobiography, *Myself When Young*, particularly the description of her mediocre success at the Ladies Presbyterian College in Melbourne, is for some reason inaccurate. See Leonie J. Kramer, *Myself When Laura; fact and fiction in Henry Handel Richardson's school career* (Melbourne, 1966) for this particular item and the others that follow for earlier sources:

(1) M. H. Clutton-Brock, "Mrs. Lins: Sister to Henry Handel Richardson," *Southerly* 27, no. 1 (Winter, 1966), 46–59. A detailed, affectionate account of Mrs. Lins's growing to womanhood, marriage, and life as it crossed Henry Handel Richardson's, stressing the closeness of the sisters and Mrs. Lins's involvement in Summerhill, A. S. Neill's school.

(2) Uther Barker, "Epitaph of a Novelist," *Southerly* 10, no. 2 (Winter, 1949) 89–92. A perceptive, critical review of the stylistic weaknesses, brevity, and "Impression of being written by another hand" of *Myself When Young*, with an appreciation of Robertson's "The Art of Henry Handel Richardson."

(3) Alice Henry, "Who is Henry Handel Richardson?" *Bookman* (New York) 70 (December 1929), 355–59.

(4) Jane Mander, "Henry Handel Richardson," *Bookman* (London) 76 (May, 1929), 104–5.

(5) Colin Arthur Roderick, "The Personality of Henry Handel Richardson," *Australian Quarterly* 20 (December, 1948), 44–45.

(6) Nettie Palmer, *Henry Handel Richardson: A Study* (Sydney, 1950).

(7) Edna Purdy and Olga M. Roncoroni, eds., *Henry Handel Richardson: Some Personal Impressions* (Sydney, 1957).

(8) Vincent Buckley, *Henry Handel Richardson* (Melbourne, 1961).

(9) Leonie Kramer, *Henry Handel Richardson* (Melbourne, 1967).

(10) National Trust of Australia (Victoria), *Henry Handel Richardson Memorial; Lake View Chiltern* (Melbourne, 1969).

20. Palmer, p. 11.

21. Richardson, *Myself When Young*, p. 9.

22. Alan Stoller and R. H. Emmerson, "The Fortunes of Walter Lindesay Richardson," p. 33.

23. Richardson, *Myself When Young*, p. 11.

24. *Ibid.*, p. 13.

25. Ms. 133/47 Walter Lindesay Richardson correspondence, National Library, Canberra and Stoller and Emmerson, "Richard Mahony, Walter Lindesay Richardson, and the Spirochaete."

26. Walter Lindesay Richardson, Chiltern Letters, no. 12, Ms. 133/47, National Library, Canberra.

27. *Ibid.*, no. 10 (Ms. 133/47).

28. Frost Letters, Ms. 133/79, National Library, Canberra.

29. *Ibid.*

30. Richardson, *Myself When Young*, p. 20.

31. Stoller and Emmerson, "Richard Mahony, Walter Lindesay Richardson and the Spirochaete," p. 19.

32. Richardson, *Myself When Young*, p. 21.

33. *Ibid.*, p. 23.

34. *Ibid.*, p. 24.

35. Yarra Bend Records of Dr. Richardson, the Moir Collection, State Library of Victoria, La Trobe University, Melbourne.

36. See Stoller and Emmerson, "General Paralysis in Victoria: An Historical Study," *Medical Journal of Australia* 2 (1969), p. 607; Cecil H. Hadgraft, "Diagnosis of Mahony," *Australian Quarterly* 27 (June, 1955), 87–95. Morris E. Miller, "Richard Mahony's Euphoria: a psychological note,' *Meanjin Quarterly* 11 (Summer, 1952) pp. 397–401.

37. Yarra Bend Records, Moir Collection, State Library of Victoria.

38. Richardson, *Myself When Young*, p. 24.

39. Dorothy Green, Walter Lindesay Richardson: the Man, the Portrait, and the Artist," *Meanjin Quarterly* 29 (Autumn, 1970), 19.

40. Richardson, *Myself When Young*, p. 24.

41. *Ibid.*, p. 27.

42. From the correspondence between Rupp and Miller, Moir Collection, La Trobe Library, Melbourne.

43. Richardson, *Myself When Young*, p. 27.

44. E. Morris Miller, "Richard Mahony's Grave," *Meanjin Quarterly* 8 (Spring, 1949), 178.

45. Richardson, *Myself When Young*, p. 33.

46. *Ibid.*, p. 35.

47. Some dispute exists whether she was twelve or thirteen, but her first attendance mark in the school records indicates she was thirteen, despite her own account in *Myself When Young*. See Leonie Kramer, *Myself When Laura* (Melbourne, 1966), p. 4.

48. Richardson, *Myself When Young*, pp. 65, 66, 69; and Kathleen Fitzpatrick, draft copy of a centenary history of the Presbyterian Ladies College, p. 12 (to be published in Melbourne, 1975).

49. Richardson, *Myself When Young*, p. 70.

50. 1887 Diary, National Library of Australia, Ms. 133, item 56.

51. Richardson, *Myself When Young*, p. 67.

52. *The Melbourne Age*, January 18, 1886, p. 12.

53. Kramer, *Myself When Laura*, p. 8.

54. National Library of Australia, Ms. 113, item 54.

55. Kramer, *Myself When Laura*, p. 9.

56. Richardson, *Myself When Young*, p. 73.

57. Nettie Palmer, *Henry Handel Richardson* (Sydney, 1950), p. 19.

58. Green, *Ulysses Bound* (Canberra, 1973), p. 23; and Green, "A Poet in Prose Who Saw 'With Energy,'" *Hemisphere* 13 (November, 1969), p. 23.

59. Catherine Boys to Mrs. W. L. Richardson, July 9, 1884, W. L. Richardson Papers, Letters, "Miscellaneous," Ms. 133/47.

60. Olga Roncoroni, by interview, St. Leonards, England, March 27, 1974, and Ms. 133, Item 80 in the National Library, Canberra.

61. Richardson, *Myself When Young*, p. 91.

62. *Ibid.*, pp. 95, 74. This verifies Mrs. Richardson's intent, encouraged by the staff at Ladies Presbyterian College, to follow through on the talents of her daughter. It also justifies the author's account in her autobiography that it was a "relative-visiting" trip, that in fact her mother had intended after selling the Hawthorn house to "take us 'home' for a trip," to show off "her two girls—the one for her reputed cleverness, the other for her good looks."

63. *Ibid.*, p. 74.

64. *Ibid.*, p. 98.

65. Leonie Kramer, *Henry Handel Richardson* (Melbourne, 1967), p. 13; and Green, *Ulysses Bound* (Canberra, 1973), p. 23.

66. National Library of Australia, Ms. 133, Items 43–45.

67. National Library of Australia. Ms. 133, Items 16–17.

68. Dorothy Green indicates that a "disfiguring birthmark down her right arm" might have added to the terror of public appearances. *Ulysses Bound*, p. 23, footnote 9.

69. Richardson, *Myself When Young*, p. 116.

70. *Ibid.*, p. 117.

71. *Ibid.*, p. 120.

72. *Ibid.*

73. *Ibid.*, p. 121.

74. *Ibid.*, p. 122.

75. *Ibid.*, p. 123.

76. *Ibid.*, p. 125.

77. *Ibid.*

78. *Ibid.*, p. 126.

79. See Kramer, "Henry Handel Richardson: the Limits of Realism," *Melbourne Critical Review* 3 (Spring, 1960), 75–79; T. Inglis Moore, "The Misfortunes of Henry Handel Richardson," Commonwealth Literary Fund Lectures (1957) and letters in the Palmer papers, Australian National Library, Canberra. Information also obtained by personal interview with Leonie Kramer, Canberra, April 14, 1974.

80. Kramer, "Henry Handel Richardson: The Limits of Realism," p. 75.

81. Henry Handel Richardson, "Early Prose Attempts," Ms. 133, item 60, Australian National Library. Canberra.

82. *Ibid.*, p. 1.

83. *Ibid.*

84. 1897 Diary. Ms. 133, item 90, Australian National Library. Canberra.

85. "Notes on Mother's Last Illness and Death," Ms. 133, item 60, Australian National Library, Canberra.

86. Henry Handel Richardson, First letter to her father, 1874. Ms. 133, item 53, Australian National Library, Canberra.

87. *Ibid.*

88. "Notes on Mother's Last Illness and Death," Ms. 133, item 60.

89. 1897 diary, Ms. 133, item 90.

90. Henry Handel Richardson, preface to *Niels Lyhne* (London. 1897), p. iii.

91. Dorothy Green seems to consider this a strong possibility in *Ulysses Bound* (Canberra, 1973), p. 544.

92. Henry Handel Richardson 1897 and 1898 diary, Ms. 133, item 90, Australian National Library, Canberra.

93. Henry Handel Richardson, 1901 diary, Ms. 133, item 90, Australian National Library, Canberra.

94. Green, *Ulysses Bound,* p. 546.

95. 1887 notebook, Ms. 133, item 90, Australian National Library, Canberra.

96. 1902 notebook, Ms. 133, item 90, Australian National Library, Canberra.

97. J. G. Robertson, "Notes" in Henry Handel Richardson, *Myself When Young,* edited by Olga M. Roncoroni (London, 1950), pp. 149–50.

98. Henry Handel Richardson, "Some Notes on My Books," in *Southerly* 23, no. 1 (1963), 9.

99. *Ibid.,* p. 10.

100. Ms. 133, item 2, The Australian National Library, Canberra.

101. Richardson, "Some Notes on My Books," p. 11.

102. *Ibid.*

103. *The Australian Encyclopedia* (East Lansing; Michigan State University Press, 1958), p. 424.

104. Richardson, "Some Notes on My Books," p. 11.

105. J. G. Robertson Papers (1896–1926), Ms. 133, box 8, Australian National Library, Canberra.

106. J. G. Robertson, "The Art of Henry Handel Richardson," in Henry Handel Richardson, *Myself When Young* (London, 1948), p. 164.

107. Richardson, "Some Notes on My Books," p. 12.

108. Henry Handel Richardson, "My Favorite Authors," Ms. 133, item 72, Australian National Library, Canberra.

109. Richardson, "Some Notes on My Books," pp. 13–14.

110. Edna Purdie and Olga M. Roncoroni, eds., *Henry Handel Richardson, Some Personal Impressions* (Sydney: Angus and Robertson, 1950), p. 73.

111. "Preliminary notes for *The Fortunes of Richard Mahony,*" Ms. 133, item 10A, The Australian National Library, Canberra.

112. 1912 diary, Ms. 133, item 10B, Australian National Library, Canberra.

113. *Ibid.*

114. *Ibid.*

115. Interview with Professor Kramer, April 24, 1974, Canberra.

116. Richardson, "Some Notes on My Books," p. 15.

117. *Ibid.*, p. 16.

118. Walter Lindesay Neustatter, "Impressions," in Purdie and Roncoroni, *Henry Handel Richardson: Some Personal Impressions*, p. 86.

119. Richardson, "Some Notes on My Books," p. 17.

120. Nettie Palmer, "VI," in Purdie and Roncoroni, eds., *Henry Handel Richardson: Some Personal Impressions*.

121. The Palmer Papers, Henry Handel Richardson to Nettie Palmer, December 15, 1927, Ms. 1174, item 3044, Australian National Library, Canberra.

122. "J.G.R.'s criticism of HHR's books," Ms. 133, item 61, box 8, Australian National Library, Canberra.

123. Personal interview, Professor Manning Clarke, April 16, 1974, Australian National University, Canberra.

124. Richardson, "Some Notes on My Books," p. 18.

125. This figure obtained through interview with Miss Olga Roncoroni, St. Leonards, March 27, 1974.

126. Green, *Ulysses Bound*, p. 510.

127. *Ibid.*, p. 497.

128. Interview with Olga Roncoroni, St. Leonards, March 27, 1974.

129. Critique of "Death" in T. H. Lawrence to Jacob Schwartz, April 26, 1932, Ms. 133, item 69, box 9, Australian National Library, Canberra.

130. Purdie and Roncoroni, eds., *Personal Impressions*, p. 141.

131. Interview, Olga Roncoroni, St. Leonards, March 27, 1974.

132. Leonie Kramer, *Henry Handel Richardson* (Melbourne, 1967), p. 27.

133. Letter to Miss Kathleen Ussher, December 24, 1942, The Mitchell Library, Sydney, Australia.

134. Diary Notes, Ms. 133, item 78, Australian National Library, Canberra.

135. 1941 notebook, Ms. 133, item 81, box 11, Australian National Library, Canberra.

136. Green, *Ulysses Bound*, p. 479.

Chapter Two

1. J. P. Jacobsen, *Siren Voices: Niels Lyhne*, trans. E. F. L. Robertson (London, 1898).

2. Björnstjerne Björnson, *The Fisher Lass* (London, 1898).

3. Mentioned in *Myself When Young*, p. 124.

4. *Ibid.*

5. Hanna Astrup Larsen, Introduction to *Niels Lyhne* by J. P. Jacobsen (New York, 1919), p. v.

6. Henry Handel Richardson, *Myself When Young* (London, 1950), p. 125.

7. Henry Handel Richardson, Preface to *Niels Lyhne*, Ms. 133, item 1, p. 3, Australian National Library, Canberra.

8. H. H. Richardson, "A Danish Poet,' in *Southerly* 23, no. 1 (1963), 40.

9. Dorothy Green's *Ulysses Bound* is the most thorough, but there are also a number of critics Green labels too harshly as the "literal-minded school," such as Leonie Kramer, Vincent Buckley, and Elizabeth Loder.

10. Green, *Ulysses Bound*, p. 52.

11. Edmund Gosse, Introduction to *Siren Voices: Niels Lyhne*, by Jans Peter Jacobsen, trans. E. F. L. Robertson (London, 1896), p. xiii.

12. *Niels Lyhne*, trans. E. F. L. Robertson, p. 51.

13. Green, *Ulysses Bound*, pp. 52–53.

14. *Niels Lyhne*, p. 151.

15. *Ibid.*, p. 160.

16. Green, p. 53.

17. 1941 Notebook, item 133/81, box 11, The Australian National Library, Canberra.

18. Letter from Green Ridges, Fairlight, in possession of William Heinemann, Inc. of London and photocopied through the kind permission of Mrs. Elizabeth Anderson, copyrights editor.

19. Green, p. 54.

20. *Ibid.*, pp. 51–64.

21. Richardson, *Myself When Young* (London, 1950), p. 126.

22. Henry Handel Richardson, "Ibsen in Translation," *Speaker* (London), July 10, 1897, pp. 41–42.

23. Henry Handel Richardson, "Some Notes on My Books," in *Southerly* 23, no. 1 (1963), 11.

24. Karl-Johan Rossing, ed. *Letters of Henry Handel Richardson to Nettie Palmer* (Uppsala, 1953), p. 18.

25. Dymphna Clark, "The Aurora Borealis: Henry Handel Richardson as a Translator,' *Henry Handel Richardson: 1870–1946; Papers Presented at a Centenary Seminar* (Canberra, 1972), pp. 28–29.

26. *Ibid.*, p. 29.

27. *Ibid,.* p. 30.

28. *Ibid.*, p. 32.

29. Professor Leonie Kramer, Professor of Australian Literature, University of Sydney, by personal interview in Canberra, April 10, 1974. Professor A. D. Hope was also present at the interview and concurred with Professor Kramer's statement.

30. Elizabeth Loder Webby, "Review of Dorothy Green's *Ulysses Bound*," *Southerly* 51, no. 3 (March, 1974), 76.

31. See especially the original manuscript draft, in pencil, of *Ultima Thule* (Ms. no. 133/9, box 3). The drafts are written on small sheets of paper, a paragraph at a time, with stylistic revisions that are so numerous they often make the pages indecipherable. The final copy from which the book was printed (Ms. 133/8, box 3) shows more revision.

32. Ms. 133/2, box 1, p. 2.

33. Ms. 133/2, box 1, p. 348.

34. Ms. 133/2, box 1, p. 408.

35. Clark, p. 33.

36. Henry Handel Richardson, "Autobiographical Sketch," *Twentieth Century Authors* (New York, 1942), pp. 1170–71.

37. Henry Handel Richardson, "Some Notes on My Books," in *Southerly* 23, no. 1 (1963), 9.

38. *Ibid.*, p. 164.

39. Leonie Kramer, Introduction to *Australia Felix* (Sydney, 1973), p. xiii, and William D. Elliott, "French Influences in the Novels of Henry Handel Richardson," *Discourse* 11 (Winter, 1968), 108–15.

40. Green, p. 47.

Chapter Three

1. Henry Handel Richardson, *Maurice Guest* (New York, 1930), p. 27. (All references to *Maurice Guest* will be made to this edition.)

2. *Ibid.*, p. 565.

3. *Ibid.*

4. Dorothy Green, *Ulysses Bound* (Canberra, 1973), p. 125.

5. Nettie Palmer, *Henry Handel Richardson: A Study* (Sydney, 1950), p. 57.

6. A. D. Hope, "Henry Handel Richardson's *Maurice Guest*," *Meanjin Quarterly* 24 (Winter, 1955), 186.

7. J. G. Robertson, "The Art of Henry Handel Richardson," in *Myself When Young*, by Henry Handel Richardson (London, 1948), 155.

8. Henry Handel Richardson, Introduction to *Niels Lyhne*, unpublished manuscript 133/1, National Library, Canberra.

9. Leonie Kramer, "Henry Handel Richardson," in *The Literature of Australia*, ed. Geoffrey Dutton (Melbourne, 1964), p. 329.

10. Richardson, *Maurice Guest*, p. 14.

11. *Ibid.*, p. 4.

12. *Ibid.*, p. 5.

13. *Ibid.*, p. 6

14. *Ibid.*

15. *Ibid.*, p. 10.

16. *Ibid.*, p. 12.

17. Henry Handel Richardson, "Music Study in Leipzig," *Southerly* 23, no. 1 (1963), 33–39.

18. Richardson, *Maurice Guest*, p. 14.

19. *Ibid.*, p. 16.

20. *Ibid.*, p. 17.

21. *Ibid.*, p. 20.

22. *Ibid.*, p. 27.

23. Elizabeth Odeen, *Maurice Guest: A Study*, M.A. thesis, University of Texas 1963, p. 23.

24. Richardson, *Maurice Guest*, pp. 28–29.

25. Elizabeth Loder, "*Maurice Guest*: Some Nineteenth Progenitors," *Southerly* 26, no. 11 (1966), 95.

26. 1887 diary, Ms. 133/56, Australian National Library, Canberra.

27. Leonie Kramer, *Henry Handel Richardson* (Melbourne, 1967), p. 29.

28. Dorothy Green, *Ulysses Bound* (Canberra, 1973), p. 547.

29. Richardson, *Maurice Guest*, p. 42.

30. Manning Clarke, Professor of Australian History, by personal interview at the Department of History, Australian National University, April 16, 1974.

31. Richardson, "Some Notes on My Books," *Southerly* 23, no. 1, (1963), 9.

32. William Elliott, "French Influences in *The Fortunes of Richard Mahony*," *Discourse* 11, no. 1 (Winter, 1968), 109.

33. Richardson, "Some Notes on My Books," pp. 10–11.

34. Loder, p. 95.

35. Hope, pp. 186–99.

Chapter Four

1. Dorothy Green, *Ulysses Bound* (Canberra, 1973), p. 227 indicates that Laura thought of herself as neither a writer nor a musician at the end of the novel.

2. Leonie Kramer, *Myself When Laura: Fact and Fiction in Henry Handel Richardson's School Career* (Melbourne, 1966), p. 14. I am indebted to Professor Kramer for intensive discussion about this book.

3. Henry Handel Richardson, *The Getting of Wisdom* (New York, 1931), p. 97. All references to *The Getting of Wisdom* will be made to this edition.

4. Green, p. 223.

5. *Ibid.*, p. 240.

6. *Ibid.*, p. 231.

7. Richardson, *The Getting of Wisdom*, p. 206.

8. *Ibid.*, pp. 13–14.

9. Kramer, *Myself When Laura*, p. 17.

10. Green, p. 513.

11. Kramer, p. 17.

12. Richardson, *The Getting of Wisdom*, p. 227.

13. *Ibid.*, p. 19.

14. Green, p. 239.

15. Richardson, *The Getting of Wisdom*, p. 248.

16. *Ibid.*, p. 256.

17. *Ibid.*, p. 265.

18. *Ibid.*, p. 25.

19. Henry Handel Richardson, "Some Notes on My Books," in *Southerly* 23, no. 1 (1963), 13.

20. There is some disagreement on this by the two major Richardson critics. See Kramer, "A Writer in the Making," in *Myself When Laura*, and Green, "An Engrossing Portrait,' in *Ulysses Bound*. Other critics add to the argument.

Chapter Five

1. E. M. Forster, *Aspects of the Novel* (New York, 1972), p. 6.

2. Henry Handel Richardson, *The Fortunes of Richard Mahony, Australia Felix* (New York, 1962), p. 377. All references will be made to the Norton Library edition with each volume—*Australia Felix, The Way Home,* and *Ultima Thule*—published separately.

3. *Ibid.*

4. *Ibid.*, pp. 220–21.

5. Henry Handel Richardson, "Some Notes on My Books," *The Virginia Quarterly Review* 16, no. 3 (Summer, 1940), 342.

6. Nettie Palmer, *Henry Handel Richardson: A Study* (Sydney, 1950), p. 71.

7. William Bramwell Withers, *The History of Ballarat from the First Pastoral Settlement to the Present Time* (Ballarat, 1887); and Carboni Raffaello, *The Eureka Stockade* (Melbourne, 1855).

8. Leonie J. Gibson, *Henry Handel Richardson and Some of Her Sources* (Melbourne, 1954), p. 44.

9. William Howitt, *Land, Labour and Gold; or Two Years in Victoria, etc., with Visits to Sydney and Van Diemen's Land* (London, 1958); William Kelley, *Life in Victoria; or, Victoria in 1853*

and ... in 1858 (London, 1889); Gibson, pp. 45–46; and Ms. 133/10, The National Library, Canberra.

10. Gibson, p. 23; in notebook 2, p. 146, Ms. 133/10, The National Library, Canberra.

11. C. Clacy, *A Lady's Visit to the Gold Diggings of Australia in 1852–53* (London, 1853), from her use of it in Ms. 133/10, The National Library, Canberra.

12. Withers, pp. 8–9.

13. Clacy, p. 246.

14. *Ibid.*, p. 76.

15. Henry Handel Richardson, "Some Notes on My Books," in *Southerly* 23, no. 1 (1963), 17.

16. Richardson, *The Way Home.* p. 212.

17. *Ibid.*, p. 215.

18. *Ibid.*, p. 216.

19. *Ibid.*, p. 270.

20. *Ibid.*, p. 92.

21. *Ibid.*, p. 93.

22. *Ibid.*, p. 40.

23. *Ibid.*, p. 127.

24. *Ibid.*, p. 128.

25. *Ibid.*, p. 276.

26. *Ibid.*, p. 15.

27. Richardson, *Ultima Thule*, pp. 139–40.

28. Richardson, *The Way Home,* p. 94.

29. Richardson, *Australia Felix,* p. 350.

Chapter Six

1. Dorothy Green, *Ulysses Bound* (Canberra, 1973), p. 390.

2. *Ibid.*, p. 400.

3. *Ibid.*, p. 402.

4. *Ibid.*

5. Henry Handel Richardson, *The End of a Childhood* (Norton, 1934), p. 52.

6. *Ibid.*, p. 76.

7. *Ibid.*, p. 79.

8. *Ibid.*, p. 139.

9. Nettie Palmer, *Henry Handel Richardson* (Sydney, 1950), p. 131.

10. Richardson, *The End of a Childhood,* p. 86.

11. *Ibid.*, p. 88.

12. *Ibid.*

13. *Ibid.,* p. 132. Dorothy Green discusses the obvious voyeurism in the less than objective point of view in the story. This may be of biographical interest, since it is one of the few stories when Henry Handel Richardson departs from a realist's objectivity. (*Ulysses Bound,* p. 407).

14. Richardson, *The End of a Childhood,* p. 150.

15. *Ibid.,* p. 193.

16. *Ibid.,* p. 233.

17. *Ibid.,* p. 234.

18. Green, p. 415.

19. Richardson, *The End of a Childhood,* pp. 291–92.

20. Green, *Ulysses Bound,* p. 417.

21. Henry Handel Richardson, "Death," *English Review* (London) 9 (October, 1911), 405–12.

22. Henry Handel Richardson, *Two Studies* (London, 1931).

23. Richardson, *The End of a Childhood,* p. 309.

24. *Ibid.*

25. *Ibid.,* pp. 311–12.

26. Green, p. 420.

27. Ms. letter, item 133/69, box 9, The National Library, Canberra, Australia.

28. *Ibid.*

29. *Ibid.*

30. Leonie Kramer, "Henry Handel Richardson," *The Literature of Australia,* ed. Geoffrey Dutton (Sydney, 1964), p. 327.

31. Vincent Buckley, *Henry Handel Richardson* (Melbourne, 1963), p. 8.

32. Henry Handel Richardson, "The Coat," *Good Housekeeping* (London) 36 (February, 1940), 20–21, 75–78.

33. Henry Handel Richardson, "Sister Ann," reprinted in *Southerly* 23, no. 1 (1963), 21–32.

34. Green, p. 467. Dr. F. S. B. Smith, Department of History, Social Sciences Institute, The Australian National University, indicated by correspondence that Dorothy Green's synopsis of spiritualism as used in Richardson is extremely complete.

35. Green, pp. 467, 468.

36. Richardson, "The Coat," in *Southerly* 23, no. 1 (1963), 61.

37. *Ibid.,* p. 61.

38. Richardson, "Sister Ann," 32.

Chapter Seven

1. Henry Handel Richardson, *The Young Cosima* (New York, 1934), p. 154.

2. Nettie Palmer, *Henry Handel Richardson* (Sydney, 1950), p. 138.

3. Richardson, *The Young Cosima,* p. 327.

4. *Ibid.,* p. 381.

5. *Ibid.,* pp. 355–56.

6. *Ibid.,* pp. 379–80.

7. *Ibid.,* p. 387.

8. *Ibid.,* p. 388.

9. *Ibid.*

10. Karl-Johan Rossing, ed., *Letters of Henry Handel Richardson to Nettie Palmer* (Uppsala, 1953), p. 35.

11. *Ibid.*

12. Dorothy Green, "*The Young Cosima,*" *Australian Literary Studies* 4 (May, 1969), p. 215.

13. Dorothy Green, *Ulysses Bound* (Canberra, 1973), p. 428.

14. Leonie Kramer, Introduction to Henry Handel Richardson, *The Fortunes of Richard Mahony* (Sydney, 1971), p. ix.

15. Personal interview with Professor Kramer, April 10, 1974, Canberra; Leonie Kramer, *Henry Handel Richardson* (Melbourne, 1967); Leonie Kramer, "Henry Handel Richardson," *The Literature of Australia,* ed. Geoffrey Dutton (Victoria, 1964).

16. Interview with Olga R. Roncoroni, St. Leonards, England, March 27, 1974.

17. Edna Purdie and Olga M. Roncoroni, eds., *Henry Handel Richardson: Some Personal Impressions* (Sydney, 1957), p. 87.

18. L. A. Triebel, "Source Material for *The Young Cosima,*" *Meanjin Quarterly* 14 (Winter, 1955), 201.

19. *Ibid.*

20. Dorothy Green, "*The Young Cosima,*" *Australian Literary Studies* 4 (May, 1970), 219.

21. *The Young Cosima,* p. 301.

22. *Ibid.,* p. 42.

23. *Ibid.,* p. 235.

24. *Ibid.*

25. Green, "*The Young Cosima,*" p. 223.

26. Maria Davenport, in the *New York Times Book Review,* August 10, 1969, p. 45.

27. Green, "*The Young Cosima,*" p. 224 and *passim.*

Chapter Eight

1. Cecil Hadgraft, *Australian Literature* (London: Heinemann, 1960), p. 150.

2. With Leonie Kramer's *Henry Handel Richardson and Some of her Sources* (Melbourne, 1954).

3. See F. H. Mares, *Meanjin Quarterly* 21, no. 1 (1962) 64–70; and Dorothy Green's periodical publications.

4. F. A. Swinnerton. *The Younger Novelists.* 4. *Henry Handel Richardson in the Georgian Scene; a literary panorama* (New York, Farrar and Reinhart, 1934), pp. 290–92 and *passim.*

5. Interview with Leonie Kramer, April 10, 1974, the Australian National University, Canberra.

6. By correspondence with Dorothy Green, letter from Enfield, England, June 1, 1974.

7. Interview with Leonie Kramer, April 10, 1974.

8. Dorothy Green to William D. Elliott, June 1, 1974.

9. Interview with Vincent Buckley, University of Melbourne, Melbourne, Australia, April 22, 1974.

10. Interview with C. B. Christesen, University of Melbourne offices of *Meanjin Quarterly* (April, 1974).

11. Elizabeth Loder Webby, "Review of Dorothy Green's *Ulysses Bound,*" *Southerly* 51, no. 3 (March, 1974), 76.

Selected Bibliography

PRIMARY SOURCES

1. Novels

Maurice Guest. London: Heinemann, 1908.
The Getting of Wisdom. London: Heinemann, 1910.
Australia Felix. London: Heinemann, 1917.
The Way Home. London: Heinemann, 1925.
The Fortunes of Richard Mahony. (Collected Edition) London: Heinemann, 1930.
The Young Cosima. London: Heinemann, 1939.

2. Short Stories

Two Studies. London: Ulysses Press, 1931.
The End of a Childhood and Other Stories. London: Heinemann, 1934.
"The Coat." *Good Housekeeping* (London) 36 (February, 1940), 20–21, 75–78.
"Sister Ann." *Good Housekeeping* (London) April, 1949. No further details known. Reprinted in *Woman's Day* (Sydney), May 22, 1950.

3. Articles

"Music Study in Leipzig." *Lady* (London), June 13, 1895, p. 774.
"The Schubert Centenary." *Speaker* (London), January 30, 1897, pp. 124–25.
"Ibsen in Translation." *Speaker* (London), July 10, 1897, pp. 41–42.
"A Danish Poet." *Cosmopolis* (London) 8, (November, 1897), 346–58.
"The Magic of the New Concert Room." *Radio Times* (London), May 10, 1929, p. 279.
"The Story of Wagner and von Bülow—and the Woman Behind Their Music." *Radio Times* (London), August 29, 1930, pp. 424–25.
"Some Notes on My Books." *Virginia Quarterly Review* 16 (Summer, 1940), 334–47.

[Autobiographical Sketch] in Kunitz, S. J. and Haycraft, H., eds., *Twentieth Century Authors*. New York: H. W. Wilson, 1942, 1170–71.

[Notes on] "Two Studies" and "The End of a Childhood." *Southerly* 23, no. 1 (1963), 19–20.

4. Autobiography

Myself When Young. New York: Norton, 1948.

5. Works translated by Henry Handel Richardson

Jacobsen, Jens Peter. *Siren Voices*. Trans. Ethel F. L. Robertson. Heinemann's International Library, vol. 19. London: Heinemann, 1896.

Björnson, Björnstjerne. *The Fisher Lass*. London: Heinemann, 1896.

6. Letters

Letters of Henry Handel Richardson to Nettie Palmer. Edited by Karl-Johan Rossing. Uppsala: Lundequistska, 1953.

SECONDARY SOURCES

The articles and books listed below constitute a selection of materials which should be interesting and useful to the reader of Henry Handel Richardson's fiction. For a much more extensive discussion of pertinent Richardson materials, the reader may consult the following bibliographies: Gay Howells, *Henry Handel Richardson: 1870–1946, A Bibliography to Honour the Centenary of Her Birth* (Canberra: National Library of Australia, 1970). While the Howells bibliography includes only brief annotations, it is the most complete and most reliable source. Verna D. Wittrock, "Henry Handel Richardson: An Annotated Bibliography of Writings about Her," *English Literature in Transition, 1880–1920* (Lafayette, Indiana) 7, no. 3 (1964), pp. 146–87. While this bibliography is ten years old, for study of the earlier secondary material on Richardson it represents the most thorough annotation. Maria S. Haynes, "Henry Handel Richardson," *Bulletin of Bibliography* (Boston) 21 (April, 1955), 130–36. As the first individual bibliography on Richardson, this listing includes a biographical sketch and bibliography with brief annotations.

ANDRAUD, ROBERT. "L'Australie dans les Romans de Henry Handel Richardson." *Etudes Anglaises* 3 (April–June, 1939), 132–141. This early study of the trilogy effectively develops Richardson's antiromantic, tragic and objective point of view, and particularly points to her avoidance of the romantic excesses of the typical bushranger and the gold seeker.

BARTLETT, NORMAN. "Pioneers of a New-World Literature." *South Atlantic Quarterly* 59 (January, 1950), 30–41. An early defense of Richardson's use of *imaginative* realism in the trilogy. Bartlett shows that her "imaginative social criticism is the Australian substitute for a poetic folklore and revolutionary nationalism."

BATE, WESTON. "From Gravel Pits to Green Point." In *Papers Presented at a Centenary Seminary: Henry Handel Richardson— 1870–1946*. Canberra: National Library of Australia, 1972, pp. 38–47. This most important study of the trilogy, based on a careful examination of the notebooks, reveals Richardson at times historically inaccurate but dramatically and imaginatively brilliant. Written by a man whose lifework has been a history of Ballarat, it finds her alterations of fact about the town and her father an intentional transformation to a "world of men gone mad, materialist and brutish, without relief." As Mr. Bate indicated in a telephone interview, she was determined to exaggerate the harshness to make her fiction a clearly creative and singular vision. There is no question here about her literal-mindedness.

BEACH, JOSEPH WARREN. *The Twentieth Century Novel: Studies in Technique.* New York: Appleton-Century-Crofts, 1932, p. 224. Beach is one of the first American critics to indicate *Ultima Thule* as a "powerful book" with "great plenty" of the "stuff of human nature and emotion," in a survey of the literature of the century.

BUCKLEY, VINCENT. *Henry Handel Richardson* (Australian Writers and their Work) Melbourne: Lansdowne Press, 1962. As one of the chief critics of the "literal-mindedness" school, Buckley finds *The Getting of Wisdom* "a minor masterpiece" and *Ultima Thule* the best of the trilogy, which he labels an "impressive failure" and a monument to the inflexibility of the naturalistic method. He defines the thematic pattern of *Maurice Guest* and *The Young Cosima* as novels with the theme of the extraordinary rights and privileges of genius.

CLARK, DYMPHNA. "The Aurora Borealis: Henry Handel Richardson as a Translator." In *Papers Presented at a Centenary Seminar: Henry Handel Richardson—1870–1946*. Canberra: National Library of Australia, 1972, pp. 23–37. This careful study of the translation of *Niels Lyhne* reveals Richardson's skill with dramatic narration and scenes that concerned emotional involvement but also her weakness with abstract prose and stylistic subtleties. The most important influence, however, was the thematic influence the book itself had on her own later writing; Jacobsen's method—romanticism imbued with the scientific spirit and essentially based on realism—and the effect the book had on her decision to become a writer with all the solitariness that implied.

CLUTTON-BROCK, M. A. "Mrs. Lins: Sister to Henry Handel Richardson." *Southerly* 27 (1966), 46–59. A thorough biographical account of the relationship between Henry Handel Richardson and her sister from their arrival in London as girls in 1888 until Lil's involvement in the educational projects of her second husband (A. S. Neill) at Summerhill. In light of Dorothy Green's account of the importance of early sibling rivalry between them, this is a noteworthy study.

————. "The Melancholy Optimist: An Account of Walter Lindesay Richardson and his Family." *Meanjin Quarterly* 29, no. 2 (1970), 192–208. This essay has a number of valuable details about the influence Richardson's mother had in shaping his personality.

CONNALLY, G. K. "The Classic Australian Three-Decker: A New Consideration of *The Fortunes of Richard Mahony*." *Southerly* 19, no. 3 (1958), 145–54. An interpretation of the trilogy in terms of its influences drawn from the Australian trilogy and its European models.

DALLIMORE, JENNIFER. "The Malaise of Richard Mahony." *Quadrant* 5 (Spring, 1961), 51–59. A review of Mahony's decline, mental and physical, and its relationships.

DUTTON, GEOFFREY. "Gentlemen vs. Liars." *Quadrant* 9, no. 1 (1965), 14–20. A comparative study of the gentleman in the history of the Australian novel in contrast to the "noble bushman, the sturdy shearer or any simply, homegrown Australian," with the startling conclusion that "In all Australian fiction, the slowest and cruelest destruction of a gentleman is in *The Fortunes of Richard Mahony*," and "The love of Mahony's wife Mary is destroyed as thoroughly as he is himself." In other words, Mary is the "homegrown Australian" who never had a chance.

ELDERSHAW, M. BERNARD. "Two Women Novelists: Henry Handel Richardson and Katherine Susannah Prichard." In *Essays in Australian Fiction*. Melbourne: Melbourne University Press, 1938, pp. 1–23. The analysis reinforces the value of Richardson as a novelist whose books are superior in the gradual revelation of character. The trilogy, while a "black tragedy," is the best example of this but is "neither defeatist nor pessimistic."

ELLIOTT, BRIAN. "Martin Boyd: An Appreciation." *Meanjin Quarterly*

16 (Autumn, 1957), 15–22. Based on a comparison between Boyd and Richardson, this article goes on to point to the trilogy as the most effective example of the author's use of cumulative detail to create impact, while less effective stylistically and less aware than Boyd "of the problem presented by a search for truth. . . ."

ELLIOTT, WILLIAM D. "French Influences in *The Fortunes of Richard Mahony.*" *Discourse* 11 (Winter, 1968), 108–15. While Richardson indicates that her primary French influence was Flaubert, Zola's philosophical base and method seems to contribute a great deal more to her conception and execution of *The Fortunes of Richard Mahony.*

————. "H. H. Richardson: The Education of an Australian Realist." *Studies in the Novel* 4, no. 2 (Summer, 1972), 141–153. From her early experiences that forced her into a solitariness to her final years at Green Ridges, Sussex, Henry Handel Richardson's life reflects a definite intellectual and emotional development that makes her fidelity to realism understandable.

EWERS, JOHN K. *Creative Writing in Australia.* Melbourne: Georgian House, 1945, rev. ed. 1959. Sees Henry Handel Richardson as essentially a great writer of "character study," with the "perfection of detail" in a slow building process that provides the trilogy with "one of the most dramatic denouements in modern fiction."

GOULD, GERALD. *The English Novel of Today.* London: Castle, 1924, pp. 46, 152–53. Probably one of Richardson's most supportive book reviewers. In the London *Observer* he describes *The Getting of Wisdom* as the best of all contemporary school stories and *Maurice Guest* as "unique" and influential.

GRATTAN, C. HARTLEY. *Australian Literature.* Seattle: University of Washington Book Store, 1929, p. 21. One of the earliest American accounts of Richardson's work, Grattan describes *Maurice Guest* as "by far the greatest novel written by an Australian" and *The Fortunes of Richard Mahony* as a trilogy that "may overshadow every other Australian novel."

GREEN, DOROTHY. "The Pilgrim Soul: The Philosophical Structure of *The Fortunes of Richard Mahony.*" *Meanjin Quarterly* 28, (1968), 328–37. In this careful study, Green proves that Richardson regarded herself as her father's spiritualized "revived self" with the trilogy as the first Australian philosophical novel. The trilogy came from Richard Mahony's desire for change as contrasted to Mary's desire for permanence and, in doing so, created artistic virtue out of psychological necessity. She turned, as did Christopher Brennan, to the inner self to describe a love-hate relationship with both parents.

————. "The Young Cosima." *Australian Literary Studies* 4, (May, 1970), 215–26. In another carefully documented study Green claims that *The Young Cosima*, not the trilogy, shows best Richardson's concern with character and character relationships.

————. *Ulysses Bound: Henry Handel Richardson and her Fiction.* Canberra: Australian National University Press, 1973. Includes lengthy studies of her short stories and her last novel, defending the author as "an imaginative novelist, not a mere chronicler." The first full-length study of Richardson since 1950, based on an exhaustive examination of the manuscripts in the National Library.

GREEN, HENRY MACKENZIE. *Australian Literature, 1900–1950.* Melbourne: Melbourne University Press, 1951, rev. 1963. Credits the trilogy as "the highest peak of Richardson's achievement, and of the achievement of the Australian novel. . . . it is in the great tragic tradition, and upholds it."

————. *A History of Australian Literature.* Sydney: Angus and Robertson, 1961. 2 vols. This work is the recognized standard history of Australia's literature, with penetrating critical evaluations of Richardson's novels that argue for imaginative realism.

HADGRAFT, CECIL H. "Diagnosis of Mahony." *The Australian Quarterly* 27 (June, 1955), 87–95. One of the first detailed studies, based on medical evidence and reference, that discovers Mahony "as the victim of cerebral arteriosclerosis, an affliction found mostly in persons aged fifty onwards."

————. *Australian Literature, a Critical Account to 1955.* London: Heinemann, 1960. A valuable accounting of each novel, Hadgraft's analysis puts Richardson in the long European tradition and finds *Maurice Guest* her best novel, with the trilogy "powerful as it is, it is a work of pathos." Since the trilogy is drawn from a physical course of a disease and heavily autobiographical, he feels it shows her deficiency of imagination. This statement, together with Hadgraft's objection to her "awkward and clumsy traits of style" clearly place him with the Kramer and Buckley school and against Green's imaginative realism.

HESELTINE, HARRY P. "Australian Image: 1) The Literary Heritage." *Meanjin Quarterly* 21, (March, 1962), 35–49. Places *Maurice Guest* within Trilling's 1961 definition of the modernist element in literature: its characters and plotting are an expert example of the modernist writer who rejects society because it is founded on cruelty and sustained by petty rationalistic rules.

HOPE, A. D. "Henry Handel Richardson's *Maurice Guest.*" *Meanjin Quarterly* 14 (Winter, 1955), 186–99. A landmark article in two key issues that confront critical opinion since Richardson's death: her use of autobiography and her style. Hope asserts that *Maurice Guest* is a novel of musical genius written under the influence of the Nietzschean superman, despite its often moody prose and its clear writing out of her frustrated musical talent. While this article was written in 1955, Hope reaffirms this position by interview on April 10, 1974, at Canberra; he is attacked by Green in *Ulysses Bound.*

HOWARTH, R. G. "Henry Handel Richardson's *The Fortunes of Richard Mahony* and *The End of a Childhood.*" *The Australian Quarterly* 27, (March, 1955), 89–102. A detailed defense of character revelation with parallels to George Eliot's use of a gradual exposure of Mahony's fatal flaws with Romola's. Howarth also sees Mary as portrayed in *The End of a Childhood* as the victim of malevolent fate, varied by blind fortune.

JEFFARES, A. NORMAN. "Maurice Guest." *Dubliner* 1 (November–December, 1961), 3–7. Reprinted in 1965 as the introduction to the Australian edition of *Maurice Guest,* Jeffares describes the novel as "a study of sexual selection at work among artists. It presents a serious study of the moral problems sex creates for those who are at the mercy of developing talents and attempts to relate these moral problems to the workings of life itself."

————. "Richard Mahony, Exile." *Journal of Commonwealth Literature* 4, no. 6 (January, 1969), 106–19. In an intensive, novel-by-novel analysis of the trilogy, Professor Jeffares reminds us Mahony is "hunted as well as hunter, and his pursuit of freedom, financial as well as intellectual, becomes ironically and paradoxically, in the grand manner, his flight from death as well as debt." And this flight is always described in a way Joyce has written of Ireland—love and hatred of an environment "as a backdrop for a more universal interpretation of human life developed through the story of an individual."

KIERNAN, BRIAN. "Romantic Convention and *Maurice Guest.*" *Southerly* 28 (1968), 286–94. By defining *Maurice Guest* as Richardson's mature but not great novel, Kiernan defends it as a novel of love which adapts the romantic conventions of popular romance. Like no other Australian novel about love, it "sees love not as an ideal relationship with another, or as an emblem of accord with the world or beyond, but as a blind, destructive passion."

————. "The Fortunes of Richard Mahony." *Southerly* 29 (1969), 199–209. While Kiernan asserts that the proems to the first two books do not follow through events that summarize a society but lead toward the individual—Richard and Mary— "its achievement lies ultimately in Richardson's ability to see the irreconcilability of both responses—that which sees life as becoming, or seeking to become, that which sees life as being and accepting—with honesty, sympathy and detachment."

KRAMER, LEONIE J. *Henry Handel Richardson and Some of Her Sources.* Melbourne: Melbourne University Press, 1954. This landmark study of Richardson's notebooks, 1912 diary, and manuscript draft of the trilogy argues convincingly for her "literal-mindedness" in the transformation of sources into art, particularly in *Australia Felix.* Too often facts are drawn directly from a contemporary history of the time, and superficially transformed, which often results in a dull and prosy style.

————. "Henry Handel Richardson: The Limits of Realism," *Melbourne Critical Review* no. 3 (Spring, 1960), 75–79. More properly entitled the "defeat" of realism, this article is perhaps the most conclusive statement of Richardson's "inability to escape from or breathe life into her facts." Her realistic words and places, Kramer feels, are a deadening crutch that cuts off her imaginative powers.

————. *A Companion to Australia Felix.* Melbourne: Heinemann Educational Books, 1962. A general but valuable guide for the student or general reader, including the historical setting, sources of the historical material, structure and style of the book, a list of main characters, maps and illustrations.

————. "Henry Handel Richardson." In *The Literature of Australia,* ed. Geoffrey Dutton. Sydney: Penguin Books, 1964. As a chapter in a critical history of major Autsralian writers, this excellent overview asserts that, while only a portion of this expatriate writer's work is Australian, to consider her work as a whole is "to see her Australian novels in perspective." Her total work was influenced by her infatuation with *Niels Lyhne's* "romanticism imbued with the scientific spirit, and essentially based on realism." Her contribution to Australian literature is clear: she "shows in all her novels an attachment to the individual personality and to personal relationships, including moral problems and their relationships, which in Australian fiction have often been pushed into the background by landscape."

————. *Myself When Laura: Fact and Fiction in Henry Handel Richardson's School Career.* Melbourne: Heinemann, 1966. This monograph contrasts Ethel Richardson's schoolgirl career at the Presbyterian Ladies College with her portrayal of Laura Rambotham in *The Getting of Wisdom*, showing Richardson's ability to satirize the *learning* of facts over the acquisition of wisdom. Kramer also contrasts Richardson's statements in her autobiography, *Myself When Young*, with the records of her school successes available in the Australian National Library.

——————. *Henry Handel Richardson*. Melbourne: Oxford University Press, 1967. Written for the Great Australians Series. This book summarizes Kramer's position: Richardson was skilled "in reconstruction rather than in creation. Her mind was exceedingly literal, and the respect for accuracy which makes her so reliable a writer also fetters her imagination." It also defends her concept of herself as a failure and the theme of failure that predominates each work.

——————. Introduction to *The Fortunes of Richard Mahony*, by Henry Handel Richardson. Sydney: Penguin Books, 1971, pp. v–xxvii. Professor Kramer's most recent statement on Richardson provides exact parallels between Zola's method of building the naturalistic novel and Richardson's approach to the writing of *Australia Felix*. She maintains, as well, that in the history of the Australian novel, Richard Mahony still remains the first substantial character.

LEWIS, SINCLAIR. Foreword to *The Fortunes of Richard Mahony*, by Henry Handel Richardson. New York: The Press of the Reader's Club, 1941, pp. v-vii. Interesting for American readers; Lewis not only admits identification with Mahony's search for "home" but points out obvious parallels between the pioneer life of Australia, so faithfully represented in the novel, and America's pioneer past. He also ranks the trilogy with Wells's larger novels, Dreiser's *Sister Carrie*, Galsworthy's *The Forsyte Saga*, and the novels of Conrad, Lagerlof, and Hamsun.

LODER, ELIZABETH. "*Maurice Guest*: An Innocent Abroad." *Balcony* 4 (1965), 34–37. Interesting as an analysis of the first Australian edition of *Maurice Guest*, and as one of the first critical commentaries by an important Richardson scholar of the "literal-mindedness" school. Loder discovers the novel handicapped by the naturalistic method and clichés "full to the brim." The scenic irony of the novel is praised, and two most interesting characters, Krafft and Louise, stand between egotism and a longing for permanence.

——————. "The Fortunes of Richard Mahony: Dream and Nightmare." *Southerly* 25, no. 4 (1965), 251–63. Loder's is one of the best studies of imagery in the trilogy, centered around the pattern of confinement and escape.

————. "*Maurice Guest*: Some Nineteenth Progenitors." *Southerly* 26, no. 22 (1966), 94–105. Loder maintains that Richardson was influenced by the nineteenth-century continental novelists, particularly Flaubert, the theme and character of the fatal woman, Dostoevski's Raskolnikov, the Decadent Movement in general, and most specifically, *Niels Lyhne*.

MARES, F. H. "*The Fortunes of Richard Mahony*: A Reconsideration." *Meanjin Quarterly* 21 (March, 1962), 64–70. Richardson is in the tradition of the naturalistic novelists of northern Europe at the end of the nineteenth century. Her facts are always exact, but they are transformed by the imagination so that "like a stove and a chair, a picture and a pair of pistols in *Hedda Gabler*, they become suggestive of a great deal more than they simply are."

MILLER, E. MORRIS. *Australian Literature from Its Beginnings to 1935: A descriptive and Bibliographical Survey.* 2 vols. Melbourne: Melbourne University Press, 1940; 1955 (revised by F. T. Macartney), pp. 515–20, 705. As an overview, this revised sketch stresses Richardson's objectivity in *Maurice Guest* and her rationalistic and realistic approach, and it claims that *Ultima Thule* is the best of the trilogy, as it concerns itself with character and motive rather than historical events.

————. "Richard Mahony's Euphoria: A Psychological Note." *Meanjin Quarterly* 11 (Summer, 1952), 397–401. One of the early studies of Mahony's mental illness, Miller finds evidence to indicate that *Ultima Thule* reveals uncommon "psychiatric insight" into euphoria, definitely portraying "a negative, or passive" phase of it.

MILLETT, FRED B. *Contemporary British Literature.* 3d ed. New York: Harcourt Brace, 1950. Millett places Richardson at the head of realistic women novelists of the contemporary British novel.

MOORE, T. INGLIS. "The Misfortunes of Henry Handel Richardson." Commonwealth Literary Fund Lectures, 1957. Canberra: Canberra University College, 1957. An assertion of the acidity of Richardson's personality, drawn from her correspondence with Jacob Schwartz, publisher of her *Two Studies*, indicates that her detachment was a kind of selfishness that prevented her from more effective imaginative fiction. An interesting accounting of the effects of withdrawal from life during her years in London.

————. *Social Patterns in Australian Literature.* Sydney: Angus and

Robertson, 1971. Placing Richardson in the cultural tradition of Australia, Moore finds that she drew upon European naturalism for her outlook and technique, concentrated on the psychology of the individual, wrote apart from the people, and detailed unremittingly all the weaknesses of her characters.

NEW, WILLIAM H. "Convention and Freedom: A Study of *Maurice Guest.*" *English Studies* (Amsterdam, Netherlands), Anglo-American supplement, 1969, pp. lxii–lxviii. New advances the theory that the novel is a story of the failure of love but more of the failure of compromise. "Maturity lies not in the avoidance of fact, however, but in a reconciliation with it; it lies not in the separation of art from the world but in the union of the two. The separation in Maurice's case is an inability validly to assess himself."

ODEEN, ELIZABETH DUFFY. "Maurice Guest: A Study." M.A. thesis, University of Texas, 1963. A detailed study of the genesis, exposition, method, secondary criticism and comparative study with *The Young Cosima* and *The Fortunes of Richard Mahony*.

PALMER, NETTIE. *Fourteen Years: Extracts from a Private Journal*. Melbourne: Meanjin Press, 1948. An interesting record of Palmer's first meeting with Richardson, who was "diminutive yet commanding."

————. *Henry Handel Richardson: A Study*. Sydney: Angus and Robertson, 1950. The first book-length study on Richardson, Palmer begins the critical questions of this writer's work with a biographical chapter, a chapter on each of her works, and valuable use of information gained from personal acquaintance with the author.

————. "Henry Handel Richardson: (I) The Writer." *Meanjin Quarterly* 7 (Spring, 1948), 154–63. Richardson's determination as a child to become a writer and her "implacable will," the importance of her husband's work in the understanding of her, and the significance of her childhood and youth were the major contributing factors in the making of a writer.

————. "Henry Handel Richardson: (II) Her Work." *Meanjin Quarterly* (Summer, 1948), 231–40. While some of this material is elaborated upon in Palmer's book-length study, she analyzes each book as significant to the whole of a rich, complex, and durable writer's work.

PHILLIPS, ARTHUR ANGELL. *The Australian Tradition: Studies in a Colonial Culture*. Melbourne: F. W. Cheshire, 1958, 77–80. Phillips describes the trilogy as "one of the best studies of the

Anglo-Australian tension." However, its real theme is "the discovery and revelation of the meaning of her father's life."

PURDIE, EDNA and OLGA M. RONCORONI, eds. *Henry Handel Richardson: Some Personal Impressions*. Sydney: Angus and Robertson, 1957. An invaluable and unique record of personal memories of Richardson by nine friends and relatives, including Arnold Gyde, a Heinemann editor; Dr. Walter Lindesay Neustatter, the author's nephew; and a long account of the author's last years by her literary executrix, Olga M. Roncoroni.

ROBERTSON, J. G. "The Art of Henry Handel Richardson: An Essay in Appreciative Criticism." In *Myself When Young* by Henry Handel Richardson. New York: W. W. Norton, 1948, 153–210. Robertson stresses the continental influences on *Maurice Guest* but calls it the greatest English naturalistic novel, the end of a chain beginning with *Madame Bovary*. *The Getting of Wisdom*, on the other hand, is indebted to Tolstoy and Björnson for its ironic comedy, whereas the trilogy is in the English tradition.

RODERICK, COLIN ARTHUR. *The Australian Novel*. Sydney: William Brooks, 1945, pp. 196–98. A rather early, "over-praising" study that is typical of first recognition, which asserts Richardson's work superior to any Australian novelists with the trilogy ranking close to *Anna Karenina* and *Madame Bovary*.

————. *An Introduction to Australian Fiction*. Sydney: Angus and Robertson, 1950, pp. 91–101. While critical of her style, Roderick concludes that "the novel of character, realistic in conception and manner, rises to preeminence in Australian literature with her work."

————. "The Personality of Henry Handel Richardson." *Australian Quarterly* 20 (December, 1948), 44–55. Written as a close critical reaction to Richardson's *Myself When Young* upon its publication, this represents a careful examination of her own personal comments, including Richardson's own attraction to a schoolgirl, mentioned in the autobiography, and its reflection in the homosexual relation between Schilsky and Krafft in *Maurice Guest*.

STEWART, KENNETH. "The Prototype of Richard Mahony." *Australian Literary Studies* 4 (May, 1970), 227–40. From an examination of the Walter Lindesay Richardson papers at the National Library, Stewart carefully examines the abundant records of Henry Handel's father to discover that she downgrades his position, heightens the nervous energy that makes him not at home either in Australia or England, and leaves out his intellectual interests and accomplishments in *The Fortunes of*

Richard Mahony. As the trilogy progresses, it becomes clear that she is exercising her "critical artistic manipulation of the novel as tragedy."

————. "Their Road to Life: A Note on Richard Mahony and Walter Richardson." *Meanjin Quarterly* 29, no. 4 (1970), 505–8. As a response to Green's thesis in *Ulysses Bound* and Dr. Stoller and Mrs. Emmerson on Walter Richardson's syphilitic condition, Stewart still maintains that physical disease or not, Richardson's prose "reveals the irritable, hypersensitive personality of a Richard Mahony." And further, the hints that these writings yield, provided the author with the keys for a perfect fusion of art and life.

STOLLER, ALAN and R. H. EMMERSON. "The Fortunes of Walter Lindesay Richardson. *Meanjin Quarterly* 1 (1970), 21–23. Both authors show conclusively that "the clinical picture as presented in the novel is that of tabo-paresis, due to syphilitic infection of the brain and spinal cord." They also prove conclusively that Richardson was indeed an imaginative realist in the portrayal of her father, since his accomplishments as a doctor show that he had a "deep sense of responsibility to his profession," and without the affliction of cerebral syphilis would have gone on to become a major figure in the development of medicine in Victoria.

TRIEBEL, L. A. "Source Material for *The Young Cosima.*" *Meanjin Quarterly* 14 (Winter, 1955), 200–2. With an appended index of the authors and biographers Richardson used as source material for *The Young Cosima,* purchased in 1947 by the University of Tasmania Library, Triebel proves how carefully the author used her sources to transform the historical materials into "imaginative" realism. He also indicates that "diaries and reminiscences of contemporaries were especially useful to this end, to which HHR's pencilled marginal notes in some of her sources bear witness."

————. *"The Young Cosima." Australian Letters: A Quarterly Review of Writing and Criticism* 5, no. 1 (1962), 53–57. Tracing the life of Wagner covered by Richardson's book in detail, Triebel concludes that Richardson "worked *The Young Cosima* on a small canvas, but intensely, with immense seriousness, absorbed in the development of essential detail." While her style "is as idiomatic and as English as Galsworthy's or Hardy's and in this novel she is rather more economical than they in the use of words . . . her imaginative power, strong sense of tragic irony and capacity for taking pains reconstructed a microcosm of human aspirations, failures and triumphs."

WALSH, WILLIAM. *Commonwealth Literature*. London: Oxford University Press, 1973. As the most recent overview of all the Commonwealth literatures, the chapter on Australia contains a brief but surprisingly thorough analysis of Richardson as "a powerful, magisterial talent, the first in Australian literature that can be fitted with propriety on an international scale." Walsh describes much of her work as Anglo-Australian, but most importantly, recognizes her as an imaginative realist: ". . . it was the creative strength of her talent which enabled her so firmly to realize the processes of growth, as they are concentrated in the young, or distributed over a whole life; it was a more poetic consciousness which enabled her to unfold the dissolution of the personality and the dismantling of the self."

Index

(The works of Henry Handel Richardson are listed under her name.)